Thinking With The Big Head

A Guide to Governance

Jamil "VA the Governor" Aaron

Thinking With The Big Head

By Jamil "VA the Governor" Aaron

ISBN-13: 978-1511442268
ISBN-10: 1511442263

First Printing, March 2015

For questions, author interviews and additional services to help Think with the Big Head contact the Governor at:

www.eyecuonline.com
vadagov@gmail.com

This book is dedicated to my parents Cynthia and Leo Aaron, my wife Melissa Aaron, and my daughters, Jamiya, Yasmeen, Isis, and Teagan Aaron. To all the men who feel lost at times when dealing with your women, this is for you. Use it to find your way. Power UP!

Acknowledgements

First and foremost, I'd like to thank my Heavenly Father and my parents in the flesh. I thank my Creators for the abilities I am blessed with and providing the environment that has allowed me to grow and bless others. I'd like to thank my Earthly Father for being my best friend during my high school years. I'd like to thank my Mother for everything she has done, from getting up at 3 a.m. to get ready for work to working two jobs to provide for me, and for being there for me the best she could through school, the military, prison, and through the process of creating this book.

I'd like to thank Mrs. Josie Pitts, Mrs. Donna Burton, Mrs. Jackie Harper, and Mrs. Charlene Stevenson for being good friends to my mother, great Aunts to me and positive role models for my daughters. Thank you to Mrs. Lorraine Hegi, Jenna Kassner and Susan Henning for being great in-laws and being a great support system for my wife and I as we struggled.

I'd like to thank Access Eye Centers for giving me an opportunity to better myself. I'd like to say thank you to Shira Hill for being a great supervisor and teacher and for giving me this opportunity to write Thinking With The Big Head.

I'd like to thank my Eye C U family. I'd like to say thank you to The Missus and Mrs. Rivera for helping with me with the writing process. I'd like to say thank you to Slimm Turna and Melvin Pitts for allowing me to be in their lives and see The Game through their eyes. Thank you Bob, for all your great wisdom.

I'd like to say thank you to Edwin, my big brother from another mother for motivating me and being a constant reminder of where I am from. I'd like to say thank you to my neighbors Tyrone and Gary Johns for being positive black fathers, and taking the time to show a young King the game. I'd also like to give a major thank you to the black fathers in my neighborhood of Lake Wilderness, Mr. Charles Pitts, Mr. Raymond Diamond, Mr. Tony Coleman, and Mr. T.L. Burton for taking on the responsibility of mentor and guide to the young black men of the community.

I'd like to say thank you to all the ladies that have come and gone in my life. Thank you for all the love you showed me and for allowing me the pleasure of being a part of your life, even if it was just for a moment.

To all young black men, please take advantage of this opportunity to learn about self. Use this book as motivation to be somebody because you know that you are somebody. The journey of life is hard, but it is much harder without the love and support of your family, especially when you created them.

Again, I'd like to thank my Heavenly Father for blessing me with this dream and my team. I'd like to say thank you for my supportive family, and for the opportunity to usher them to the highest realms of Heaven. Power UP.

Table of Contents

How to Use T.W.T.B.H.

Player's Guide

Thinking with the Big Head can be used as a guide to help The Player identify himself and give him an outline to help him grow and develop. Thinking with the Big Head can be the foundation that The Player uses to build upon, the understanding he can lean upon during tough times, and a guide to help him make decisions. The wisdom contained within Thinking with the Big Head is provided to bring light to a situation The Player may face that can change his life. Thinking with the Big Head provides The Player with the Jewels he needs to make the hard decisions, and the understanding to know that everything will work out for his benefit.

Teacher's Guide

Thinking with the Big Head can be used as a guide to teach young men the consequences of thinking with their little head. Putting T.W.T.B.H. in the hands of a young man can be life enhancing. It will act as a source of wise sayings that will give the students a manual on making good decisions. Thinking with the Big Head can act as a source material that can be quoted to bring a student understanding when he makes a mistake.

Parent's Guide

Thinking with the Big Head can be used as a guide for parents. It breaks down the lessons that a young black man needs to learn in a way they can understand. The book, combined with the online videos, will provide a single parent with the information needed to help guide their child in the right direction. The book will give insights into the challenges faced by young men in this current day as well as advice in a manner in which young men will be receptive.

Cheat Sheet

Thinking with the Big Head contains strategies that give insight into the thoughts, words and maneuvers of women. A reader could use these strategies to understand the methods and tactics of the women in his life. A reader could also learn how to deal with problems dealing with women. A reader can learn how to have a woman choose him for his best qualities and help him achieve his goals and dreams. And most importantly, the reader can learn how to avoid child support, court cases, and a violent woman.

Tools Needed for Success

Thinking With The Big Head
Journal
Pen
Calendar
An Open Mind

Glossary

T.W.T.B.H.: Thinking with the Big Head, Think with the Big Head, Thinks with the Big Head; Using knowledge, wisdom and understanding to play The Game of Life

POP: Power of the Penis; The power bestowed to the Player by the Creator to create life

POQ: Power of the Question; The knowledge learned from asking, and the influence that can be exhibited by asking

The Player: The man who recognizes the Game of Life and makes the decision to play to win

The Game: The culminating factors that influence decision making and the perceptions of the outcomes The Player makes while moving through the labyrinth of life

Team: The people in The Player's life who want to see him win; the people who give The Player knowledge, wisdom, understanding, and motivation, through actions, words or a combination of the two

Knowledge: Applicable information that can be used as a tool to affect a situation, for better or worse; Power

Wisdom: The use of knowledge to make informed decisions in life to better one's self or another; Action; A chosen woman

Understanding: Conceptualization of words, actions and outcomes; Perception

Path of Pain and Gain: Doing things the "hard way"; Learning from personal experience; feeling the pain and discomforts of life's lessons

Path of Knowledge, Wisdom and Understanding: Learning from others and recognizing victory; this path leads directly to success

Jewels: Individual pieces of knowledge, wisdom, and understanding. The karats and degree of purity will depend upon the applicability and potential for impact on life

God's Power or G.P.: The power of creation

Light: Spirit, a positive internal character

Seed: A piece of a Players God's Power

Demon: A choice that takes on a life of its own. The Player creates demons by making bad decisions and causing events that hinder and eventually eat away at him (i.e. having unprotected sex and the situations that come from it such as unwanted children, child support, or an evil woman in his life)

Eye of Investigation and Observation: The process of The Player taking what he sees and what he hears and developing an understanding. The Player then takes this understanding and compares it to the understanding of another. This process is undertaken in search of dissonance between what is being done and what is expected.

The Little Head: Perceiving the world through the 5 senses; a man's animal-istic nature

Jewels

To go along with the knowledge included in this guide, the teachings of King Solomon and other great minds can be found in the margins. These teachings are The Player's first Jewels. Due to the residual effects of slave culture (see Appendix A, The Willie Lynch Letter), many young black men grow up with only one parent. Included in King Solomon's lessons are letters written directly to a son from both mother and father. These words and lessons can substitute for the teaching of a missing parent. King Solomon's instruction and wisdom can be a guiding light for The Player. He will be comforted by the love and shielded in battle by the understanding contained within the wisdom of the wisest and wealthiest King of all time.

These Jewels reveal the results of certain decisions. The Player who listens to the words of King Solomon and these great minds will already know the outcome of listening to friends who ask him to partake in a robbery. King Solomon foretells what happens to the man who sleeps with another man's wife. If there are things going wrong in The Game, The Player can look to these Jewels to find any error he may be making.

"Wise men store up knowledge, but the mouth of a fool invites ruin."

Proverbs 10:14 NIV

Why Thinking with the Big Head

Thinking with the Big Head (T.W.T.B.H.) is an empowering tool to awaken the King within every black man. It will help any young black man find his purpose and help him understand his journey through life. It explains that life is about more than money, loose women, and material possessions. Those things come and go. T.W.T.B.H. describes the joys a black man can experience by being a good son, father and husband. These things last an eternity and define good character. T.W.T.B.H enables the young black man to be his best and avoid being his worst.

"It is splendid for the Wiseman to know everything, but the next best thing is not to be ignorant of himself."

Philebus
Plato

This volume of T.W.T.B.H. deals primarily with how men should govern themselves with women. This is very important. Who, where, when and why a man gives himself to a woman is very telling. Due to a number of factors, from the institution of slavery to the civil rights movement to modern day racial stereotypes, knowledge about the Power of the Penis and what happens when the art of sex is performed has been withheld from the black man in America. We were never allowed to know the empowering nature of sex and having a family because it caused problems for the slave master when it was time to sell and punish slaves. This has caused a dissonance that still exists today. Black men have never really been taught the joys of family life and its ability to create a legacy. We were never taught how to be fathers or models for our sons with the understanding that the son is an extension of the father.

The goal of T.W.T.B.H. is to awaken this feeling that has been denied the black men of this country, to provide the key that has the ability to turn a black man into a King. If a black man steps up to the plate and creates a family that he sustains with his own knowledge and wisdom every day, he will emerge as the King of his castle, the leader of his clan and the creator of a legacy. A kingship starts at home which is the most important realm in the kingdom. T.W.T.B.H. instructs men on how to be the man at home first. By being the man at home, he can become a man of the world.

"A kingdom is a nest of families and a family a small kingdom."

Proverbial Philosophy M.F. Tupper

If T.W.T.B.H. leads to Kingship, that means thinking with the little head leads to slavery. Men that refuse to use their Big Heads become slaves to women or, even worse, slaves to the system. Court cases and child support are the chains that will easily be placed upon the ankles of those who choose to go against the teachings of this book. If a man chooses to read this book and take the knowledge and turn it into wisdom, he will never have to worry about those things.

Back to the main question: Why T.W.T.B.H.?

There is a growing trend of young black men making babies and leaving single mothers to raise them. Young men are making decisions that lack morals, integrity, and commonsense, and these decisions are affecting the world at large. The actions of young men show an emerging trend of putting worldly material pleasures above family and honor. The purpose of *Thinking with the Big Head* is to provide young men with the knowledge, wisdom and understanding needed to make better decisions to curb these out-of-control trends.

Thinking with The Big Head provides a guide for men to use as they travel through life. This guide will show a man how to find his way while avoiding the setbacks and failures of those who came before. It will teach self-discipline by showing how to exercise self-control and how to control the penis.

Section 1: Introduction

The Game

Life is a Game

Life is a complex labyrinth made up of multiple paths. A labyrinth is defined as an intricate combination of paths or passages in which it is difficult to find one's way or to reach the exit. There is an energy that naturally propels a person through this labyrinth; part of it is social motivation and the other part is maturity in the physical sense. A person can choose to go through this maze with determination and eagerness or just move along slowly. An individual can choose to go through the labyrinth by instinct or by thought and calculation. The process of journeying through the labyrinth of life is referred to as The Game. A man that decides to play The Game to win is referred to as The Player.

"Give careful thought to the paths for your feet and be steadfast in all your ways. Do not turn to the right or the left; keep your foot from evil."

Proverbs 4:26 – 27 NIV

To get started, The Player must ask himself these questions:

1. Is he happy with the roles he has in life?
2. Is he happy with the way the ladies treat him in his life? Do they respect him?
3. Can he control his behavior around women?

4. Is he winning in life, achieving major goals and milestones?
5. Is he gaining understanding in life?

T.W.T.B.H. makes all these things possible. It opens the doors to the power and perception required to make these things an everyday reality.

The ultimate goal of The Game is to win in life and awaken the inner King within The Player. T.W.T.B.H. provides the basic understanding of The Game, defines the goal and outlines a strategy to win. It is a method of self-correction that will allow The Player to travel through the labyrinth of life with guidance and insight.

There Are Levels to This

In The Game, The Player is moving through a maze and he discovers that there are levels to this maze, just as the Pimp tells his assistant "there are levels to this pimpin'." In the military there are different ranks and different classes of these ranks. In sports, there are different leagues based on age and skill level. Within T.W.T.B.H. there are 3 phases: Lad, Adam, and King. Within these phases are 3 levels: Novice, Pro, and All Madden.

"The beginning of wisdom is this: Get wisdom and whatever you get, get insight. Prize her highly, and she will exalt you; she will honor you if you embrace her. She will place on your head a graceful garland; she will bestow on you a beautiful crown."

Proverbs 4:7 – 9 ESV

There are two factors that dictate which level and phase The Player is on:

1. The goal for which he is playing
2. The level of commitment the other team members have toward that goal.

The major difference in the phases of The Game is intention. The Lad Phase is for self. The Adam Phase is the practicing of self. The King Phase is the spreading and imposing the will of self.

"Our actions are judged good or evil according to our intentions."

The Thousand and One Nights Anonymous

The levels of The Game are the degrees of challenge. The Novice Level is the basic function and understanding of the principle. The Pro Level is when The Player is playing for a specific goal or in a specific situation with a clear understanding of what is at stake. The All Madden Level is when The Player is playing The Game for all the marbles in life.

For example, if The Player creates a team for himself by having a child, he now lives life for both himself and the child. With the added addition, he has to change the way The Game is played because he is no longer playing for just himself. He has to switch from short-term to long-term goals. There is now a greater need to succeed and to be the best at home, in addition to being the best in the world.

As he progresses through The Game, The Player will find that the levels and phases repeat themselves. The war is seldom won with a single victory. As he learns to T.W.T.B.H., these levels will be explored by examining many challenges he may experience on his journey to become the best – the best athlete, war hero, coworker, etc. and, most importantly, the best man, husband and father.

As The Player advances through each phase and level, The Game gets harder. But just as the challenges increase in magnitude, so do the rewards. The agony of defeat is equal to the glory of victory. The same type of structure can also be seen in video game play. Each compelling level brings a bigger reward and a harder challenge. The progression through The Game is the same.

With the ascension of levels should come a sense of confidence. These are the trophies and championship rings. As The Player ascends in phase and level, he will be rewarded stripes, hardware and ribbons, along with responsibilities. As he grows in levels in The Game, he will grow

"So I turned my mind to understand, to investigate and to search out wisdom and the scheme of things and to understand the stupidity of wickedness and the madness of folly."

Ecclesiastes 7:25 NIV

in responsibility as well as those for whom he is responsible. This is good. Each man is meant to lead a nation, and the goal is to be the best leader he can be so he can reach that King status, that level where he imposes his will, not only in his home, but upon others and the world as well.

"Kings detest wrongdoing, for a throne is established through right-eous-ness"

Proverbs 16:12 NIV

Keys to Success

Choose the Correct Path

T.W.T.B.H. is the key to maneuvering within the Labyrinth, using understanding to reach the goals that are set by the individual. While journeying through this maze, there are two ways that The Player can experience life: the Path of Pain and Gain; or the Path of Knowledge, Wisdom and Understanding. Instead of being hard headed, strive to become a wise King.

"The way of fools seems right to them, but the wise listen to advice."

Proverbs 12:15 NIV

The simplest way to see the two paths is to think of a child growing up. He has the choice to follow instructions or to do things his way. A child that seeks the rewards of listening to his parents will walk an easier path as compared to one who chooses to go against the instruction of his parents and plot and plan upon his own understanding. Following instructions is taking knowledge and wisdom that are given and putting them to use. On this path, The Player avoids the setbacks of unnecessary correction and maximizes his time because he is moving with hints, or cheats, which help him maneuver the labyrinth with ease. If he instead chooses to use his own limited understanding, he will meet a number of dead ends and need to be corrected. This is learning the hard way.

Think about the young lads who fail in school. How many of them spend their time being delinquents? How many corrected misfits will say they wish they had listened to the insight given to them when they were young? How many wish they had done better when they knew better? T.W.T.B.H. is the "know better" and The Player just needs to practice it daily to do and be better. T.W.T.B.H. is using the knowledge of those who came before us to master the relationships that present themselves in the present and the future. T.W.T.B.H. guides The Player to the Path of Knowledge, Wisdom and Understanding, helps him stay on that path and ensures that he will receive the Jewels that are bestowed along the way.

"Gold there is, and rubies in abundance, but lips that speak knowledge are a rare jewel."

Proverbs 20:15 NIV

There is no reason why a person should have to make the same mistake that his predecessors made before him, especially if the knowledge is there for him to use. According to Albert Einstein, continually doing the same thing over and over again while expecting different results is the definition of insanity.

Take for example men who have kids out of wedlock and then do not take control of the situation. This takes them down side streets that distract them from their destination.

T.W.T.B.H. is about learning and doing as much as possible without making mistakes and hitting setbacks, doing the most to receive the most for the team or the kingdom. It is a manual that can be used to break the cycle. The Player just has to want to do better and take action to do so. Reading and practicing the principles of T.W.T.B.H. is the first step in the right direction.

Here is another Path of Pain and Gain situation: a young black lad and his lady are having an argument and the lad continues to argue and say things he does not mean. He then gets intoxicated and goes to another lady's house or goes to partake in some sort of devilishment. He inevitably gets into trouble with his woman and/or the law.

"Stern discipline awaits anyone who leaves the path; the one who hates correction will die."

Proverbs 15:10 NIV

First and foremost, T.W.T.B.H. only promotes purposefully planned arguments and strictly prohibits doing something crazy afterwards out of emotion. Women argue with words. A man makes his statement, supports it with facts and stands on it with action. There is no need for the back and forth with words. If The Player is T.W.T.B.H., he takes a walk or does some type of exercise. The reasoning behind this is simple: this is the perfect time to burn off any extra energy created by the elevated heart rate that comes with passionate conversation. It is also the perfect time to think about the argument and whether he is right or wrong, and whether he expressed himself in the proper manner. T.W.T.B.H. also encourages The Player to take that energy and use it towards any goal that he seeks to create or achieve. Reading a book, writing or creating a piece of artwork are some examples. Is it hard to do? Yes! But if he is able to use the energy from the fiery times in life to grow and create, and he can make it a common practice, The Player will become great.

"Talent wins games but teamwork and intelligence wins cham-pion-ships"

Michael Jordan

How The Player chooses to live his life is up to him. He makes The Game easy or hard depending on the path he chooses. T.W.T.B.H. is the key to unlocking the levels of understanding in the labyrinth of life. It gives purpose to the journey through the maze and allows for proper appreciation of the rewards as The Player advances through each level. He can no longer use the excuse that he did not have anyone to help him understand. T.W.T.B.H. is here to give understanding to those who do not have any other source. It is here for The Player to practice and put into play so he can enjoy the rewards, and handle the pressure, that come with greatness.

Play Your Position

Life is a team sport and just as there are different phases and levels in The Game, there are different positions, or roles. The only way to win is to play in a way that is best for the team. The best for self will not cut it. It has to be done for the team because The Player does not play The Game by himself.

Teammates come in many forms. Some teammates are provided from birth; these teammates consist primarily of The Player's family. Other possible teammates include friends, co-workers, and the lady of The Player's choosing. All teammates help The Player in achieving his goals in life. The Player has to know himself, his goals, and the purpose of his teammates to understand his role on the team. Some teammates, such as parents, are there to give The Player motivation, guidance, and correction. The Player's parents may set rules that The Player disagrees with, or might issue a form of correction that causes The Player discomfort, but these actions should not be viewed as opposition on the part of the parents. On the contrary, the parents are playing their role on The Player's team by setting the guidelines of the path, motivation to show and prove, and the correction to ensure the same mistake is not made twice. Mistakes and losses are felt by both the parents and The Player. It is the commitment, loyalty, and persistence of their bond that enables the team to become better and win. The same applies when dealing with the

"Start children off on the way they should go, and even when they are old they will not turn from it."

Proverbs 22:6 NIV

chosen lady or Eve. As the foundations of commitment and loyalty are laid down, the opportunities for the two to work together to achieve goals will present themselves.

One of the greatest challenges in life is how to deal with teammates. T.W.T.B.H. provides The Player with the opportunity to learn his position and transition from playing for self to being a team player. From there, it teaches him how to ascend to become the best team player and then to team leader (if that role is sought or bestowed). By T.W.T.B.H., The Player will have the pleasure of building the best team in order to win The Game.

"An ounce of practice is worth a ton of preaching."

Gandhi

Practice makes perfect

As with any game, there are certain things that need to be done to prepare. First and foremost is **PRACTICE.** Practice is very important. Practice makes for perfection. The mental strength needed to win The Game will be gained by taking control of daily situations and building upon them, increasing mental strength the same way push-ups increase physical strength.

One example of such a practice is greeting people and asking how they are doing as The Player comes across them throughout the day. This is an exercise that is done repeatedly, just like push-ups, strengthening the brain muscle and making him a more effective player. He should practice it every day. He must be genuine and he should follow up with more questions. He should always look for a reason to give compliments. An effective player is always looking for the opportunity to say something positive to someone. Making it a habit of greeting people in this manner will increase The Player's personality, develop his character and establish his reputation as a good guy.

"I saw that wisdom is better than folly, just as light is better than darkness."

Ecclesiastes 2:13 NIV

If The Player wants to start T.W.T.B.H., he must start learning and practicing. T.W.T.B.H. requires him to better himself and this takes work and practice. Practice makes perfect. Practicing allows The Player to become a master of a given rule or principle. Practicing allows him to master the little nuances it takes to transform from good to great, from being a competitor to the best, from a winner to a champion, from a Lad to a King.

Accumulating Jewels

One of the goals of the daily exercises just discussed is to have conversations with others. T.W.T.B.H. involves using knowledge, wisdom and understanding to make decisions. The Player will gain a lot of knowledge, wisdom, and understanding throughout the day as he practices his new conversational skills. Keeping a journal is essential in order to record all those Jewels. This is especially important in the beginning so The Player can monitor his progress as he begins implementing the practices of T.W.T.B.H., just as a person who goes to the gym to train for an event brings a log to keep track of his workout and monitors his progression. It is also the place to flush thoughts and gives The Player an opportunity to talk to himself. Writing in journals is what great men and Kings do and should be practiced daily. It will become the key to The Player's legacy.

Studying and practicing T.W.T.B.H. will enable The Player to become an effective player in The Game. He will learn how to govern himself in a fashion that will bring him what he seeks without the setbacks of mistakes. He will learn how to get the most for his mind and body. By T.W.T.B.H., The Player has self-worth. He will also understand that sex is not free. He will know what he is giving and what he is getting for his mind and body. He will know what he is putting his life force into. In order to impress a man who is T.W.T.B.H., a woman must have something to offer other than physical pleasures.

"Wisdom will save you from the ways of wicked men, from men whose words are perverse, who have left the straight paths to walk in dark ways, who delight in doing wrong and rejoice in the perverseness of evil, whose paths are crooked and who are devious in their ways."

Proverbs 2:12 – 15 NIV

T.W.T.B.H will teach The Player how to interact with the women in his life – his mother, his sisters, and the ladies he comes across in his everyday experiences. The Player will learn the different degrees of being a young man and how to be his best self for his teammates. He will learn how to avoid foolish mistakes that other young lads fall victim to when making animalistic decisions. The Player who is T.W.T.B.H. will pass the tests of life and advance with the greatness of the best.

Section Review

- The ultimate goal of The Game is to become a King and create a legacy.

- The Game is set up like a labyrinth with 2 possible paths to choose from – the Path of Pain and Gain and the Path of Knowledge, Wisdom and Understanding.

- The Game gets progressively more difficult as you progress through the phases and levels. There are 3 Phases (Lad, Adam, King) and 3 Levels (Novice, Pro, All Madden).

- The keys to success are choosing the right path, teamwork makes the dream work, practice makes perfect, accumulate Jewels.

- There are several exercises that should be done daily. They consist of greeting people, asking how they are doing, providing compliments, engaging in conversation, writing in a journal.

- Accumulating Jewels is acquiring knowledge and wisdom to become an effective player.

Section 2: Creation

Then God said, "Let us make mankind in our image, in our likeness, so that they may rule over the fish in the sea and the birds in the sky, over the livestock and all the wild animals, and over all the creatures that move along the ground."(Genesis 1:26 NIV)

This section of T.W.T.B.H. looks closely at the creation of the Original Players in The Game. These players are known as Adam and his descendants as described in the Hebrew Bible. The purpose of this is to learn the origin of The Game and how to become an effective player. When The Player decides to T.W.T.B.H., he must first look to the past to learn the lessons of those that came before him. In this section, The Player will learn from the earliest stories of man. He will look to Adam, Esau, Jacob, and King Solomon for lessons that will enable him to master The Game.

As each character is discussed, they should be viewed as progressions of The Player through The Game. First is the creation of Adam, The Original Player, and the formation of his team. Then, an examination of the internal process that takes place when The Player progresses from the Lad Phase to the Adam Phase. This begins when the Player sees his hard work pay off and is outlined in the story of Esau and Jacob.

"All things are wearisome, more than one can say.

The eye never has enough of seeing, nor the ear its fill of hearing.

What has been will be again, what has been done will be done again; there is nothing new under the sun.

Is there anything of which one can say, 'Look! This is something new'?

It was here already, long ago; it was here before our time."

Ecclesiastes 1:8 – 10 NIV

Finally, The Player will look at one of Adam's most well-known descendants, King Solomon. It is important to analyze King Solomon because he embodies all that The Player strives to be. King Solomon was the King of his people, possessor of material wealth and, more importantly, the wisest of all Kings. He asked the Creator for the key and it was given. King Solomon leaves behind the thoughts and understanding of a King who possessed all the knowledge, wisdom, understanding and material wealth one could hope for. He left a road map of what to search for throughout The Game. He left clues to what is important and what is not. His teachings are discussed in detail in a later chapter entitled The Key Is Me.

"I [wisdom] was appointed from eternity, from the beginning, before the world began."

Proverbs 8:23 NIV

Throughout this section, keep in mind the following concepts:

1. The essence of the Creator is within creation.
2. The plight of those who came before us plagues us to this day. Their successes and failures have provided the knowledge and wisdom to overcome our modern day problems.
3. There should be personal investigation into these characters. The Player should continually strive to

learn the lessons from the characters as they overcome challenges or fail in their decision making. Invaluable Jewels can be found within the stories of their lives. The process of looking back at those who came before us for answers to problems and insight into the outcomes of certain decisions should continue throughout the progression of The Game.

Adam, The Original Player

Then the LORD God formed a man from the dust of the ground and breathed into his nostrils the breath of life, and the man became a living being. (Genesis 2:7 NIV)

In this story, the Creator creates a vessel out of Earth, which he names Adam, to receive light. Adam was created in the likeness of the Creator. Adam's ability to make the choice to create, and then do so, is an ability that comes directly from the likeness of the Creator. To take a thought and bring it forth through action is the process in which the Creator created Adam.

In other words, a young black Lad was created to receive the light of the Creator. This Lad was filled to the point where he was ready to bestow the light upon the world, just like the Creator. In creating his own creation, this Lad had the ability to share the light of the Creator and watch his own creation grow.

A man's family is his ultimate creation, the source of the Creator's light. It is also a reflection of the man's light. When The Player makes the decision to start a family, he is taking upon himself the power of the Creator, creating an extension of himself that is both a part of him and a

"You who are simple, gain prudence; You who are foolish, set your hearts on it. Listen, for I have trustworthy things to say; I open my lips to speak what is right. My mouth speaks what is true, for my lips detest wickedness."

Proverbs 8:5 – 7 NIV

separate being. The creation of his family is the creation of the Kingdom of Adam. It is through his family that he becomes like the Creator, providing for and protecting them just as the Creator provided for and protected Adam. By bestowing love, light, knowledge and wisdom upon his family, The Player is providing his team with the nutrients it needs to grow and make him happy. By taking upon this responsibility, he is tapping into the likeness of the Creator and using the power that was reserved for him to sustain His creations. This power gives The Player the ability to do miracles for his family, his creation.

In order to T.W.T.B.H., The Player must understand that mating with a woman has the potential to create. Sex creates, plain and simple. And it can create more than just babies. This is important because it is the first line of reasoning of a bigger concept of T.W.T.B.H.

SEX IS NOT FREE

The Player has to be conscious of the fact that sex creates. If he is not aware of this, he will create demons that will haunt him. Alternately, if he plants his seed in fertile land that supports him, The Player will grow to the highest levels of kingship.

***Churchill:* "Madam, would you sleep with me for five million pounds?" *Socialite:* "My goodness, Mr. Churchill...Well I suppose... we would have to discuss terms, of course... " *Churchill:* "Would you sleep with me for five pounds?" *Socialite:* "Mr. Churchill, what kind of woman do you think I am?!" *Churchill:* "Madam, we've already established that. Now we are haggling about the price"**

Winston Churchill

Chapter Review

- Adam was created in the likeness of the Creator out of Earth. This likeness is manifested in man's ability to think, act and create.

- Adam is able to create life (a baby or a demon) through sex with a woman.

- A man's family is his ultimate creation.

The LORD God said, "It is not good for the man to be alone. I will make a helper suitable for him."
Now the LORD God had formed out of the ground all the wild animals and all the birds in the sky. He brought them to the man to see what he would name them; and whatever the man called each living creature, that was its name.
So the man gave names to all the livestock, the birds in the sky and all the wild animals.
But for Adam no suitable helper was found.
So the LORD God caused the man to fall into a deep sleep; and while he was sleeping, he took one of the man's ribs and then closed up the place with flesh.
Then the LORD God made a woman from the rib he had taken out of the man, and he brought her to the man.
The man said,
"This is now bone of my bones
and flesh of my flesh;
she shall be called 'woman,'
for she was taken out of man." (Genesis 2:18-23)

Eve, Adam's Helper

The story of Eve and her interactions with Adam is a learning experience for the modern man. Learning and understanding the creation of Eve, The Player can understand a woman's purpose and determine how he should interact with her. Adam and Eve's story was passed down to provide men with a manual for understanding the creation of The Game, its players and their roles.

Teamwork Makes the Dream Work

In the creation story of woman, Eve was formed from the rib of Adam and intended to be his helper. She was created from him and for him. She is Adam's most important

"If you want to go fast, go alone. If you want to go far, go together."

African Proverb

teammate. This is a very important concept. Being his partner does not make her less than Adam; she is still his equal. The head is just as essential as the tail, the mouth as essential as the rectum. Both are key elements of the same system, just on opposite ends. The head leads as the tail follows and the mouth takes in while the rectum lets out. Adam takes in the light of the Creator; Eve reflects it.

Adam was given the title of ruler, or head decision maker, and Eve was created as his helper. He is given the burden of being the head. He has to feed the family and interact in the world on behalf of his family. Adam has to toil the land. This means that Adam has to work. Without work there is no purpose. Part of this work is thinking. It is up to Adam to have a plan to work and sustain the team. It is his burden.

This is where The Player makes the transition from Lad Phase to Adam Phase. Up until this point, he has simply lived life, making decisions based on immediate self-gratification. When he enters into the Adam Phase, things get more challenging. This is the challenge of greatness, not necessarily of The Game itself. The Game is what it is; it is life. It is when The Player decides to go for greatness that he experiences the consequences of Adam taking the original apple. He begins to recognize the hard work that

"The evil deeds of the wicked ensnare them; the cords of their sins hold them fast. For lack of discipline they will die, led astray by their own great folly."

Proverbs 5:22 – 23

has to be done to achieve greatness. He has to experience sacrifice, patience, and dedication to reach the top. It is no longer a given. The Player can make decisions and take fruits that make life hard or he can decide to control himself and enjoy the challenge of T.W.T.B.H. and win The Game by achieving goals, creating a legacy and becoming King.

Eve is pivotal in achieving the joys previously mentioned. She is The Player's assistant and helper. It is up to him to keep her on track and away from the serpent. To do this, he must have a plan for her to assist in. He must be able to provide substance for Eve or she will fall victim to the Serpent. An idle mind is the devil's workshop. If Eve is not focused on the plan, understanding her part, she can fall victim to the idle mind. It is up to The Player to properly communicate with Eve her importance and role in a manner she understands. It is through her help that he will become a King and she a Queen. The Player must know where he is going so he can lead Eve. If he gets confused, Eve is there to remind him but never to lead him astray. She only makes decisions based upon his understanding, not her own. The Player has the map and Eve helps him read it. Eve assists The Player in every way possible.

In return for Eve's hard work, dedication and loyalty,

Adam provides "the Life." This means it is The Player's duty to provide all of what Eve needs, and SOME of her wants. Women want everything so only wants that are not detrimental to the team can be looked to be fulfilled. The point is that The Player should provide for Eve's needs. Her needs should be a reflection of his own needs. The Player needs love, support, knowledge, wisdom, understanding, food, shelter, clothing, and water, and so does Eve. It is for The Player to provide all these things for Eve. Although Eve will provide him with love, support and understanding, it is not her responsibility to provide the rest. It is up to The Player to provide the rest for both of them. Eve may assist in providing these things for the team when necessary, but it should be based upon a plan that The Player created and uses Eve's natural attributes. The Player provides the idea, and Eve helps bring it to fruition. This is teamwork at its finest and teamwork makes the dream work.

Beware the Forbidden Fruit

When the woman saw that the tree was good for food, and that it was a delight to the eyes, and that the tree was desirable to make one wise, she took from its fruit and ate; and she gave also to her husband with her, and he ate.
Then the eyes of both of them were opened, and they knew that they were naked; and they sewed fig leaves together and made themselves loin coverings. (Genesis 3:6-7 NIV)

But the LORD God called to the man, "Where are you?"
He answered, "I heard you in the garden, and I was afraid because I was naked; so I hid."
And he said, "Who told you that you were naked? Have you eaten from the tree that I commanded you not to eat from?"
The man said, "The woman you put here with me—she gave me some fruit from the tree, and I ate it."
Then the LORD God said to the woman, "What is this you have done?"
The woman said, "The serpent deceived me, and I ate." .....
To the woman he said,
"I will make your pains in childbearing very severe;
with painful labor you will give birth to children.
Your desire will be for your husband,
and he will rule over you."
To Adam he said, "Because you listened to your wife and ate fruit from the tree about which I commanded you, 'You must not eat from it,'
"Cursed is the ground because of you;
through painful toil you will eat food from it
all the days of your life. It will produce thorns and thistles for you
and you will eat the plants of the field.
By the sweat of your brow
you will eat your food
until you return to the ground,
since from it you were taken;
for dust you are
and to dust you will return."
Adam named his wife Eve, because she would become the mother of all the living. (Genesis 3:9-20)

The second lesson to be learned from the story of Eve is that Adam will pay the price if he accepts the forbidden fruit that Eve presents him. This fruit can be a portal to a higher level of The Game, spring boarding The Player into situations he may not be ready for. If he does not do what he knows is right and, instead, listens to a woman, The Player will suffer the consequence – a difficult path in life. If he goes against the understanding of the Creator and the wisdom of loved ones by listening to a woman, life will become hard.

Eve is the experimental side of Adam. She was tricked into trying the fruit of the Tree of Knowledge of Good and Evil. She then persuaded Adam to try it. Eve has the ability to introduce The Player to things that will change his perception of life. He must be knowledgeable of what Eve is offering him. She had the ability to persuade Adam to do something the Creator told him not to do. This is a testament to her power. Her argument to convince Adam to do something he knows is wrong is only part of the story. Just as importantly, she did not know what would happen afterward. She had Adam take an action without knowing the consequences of the action. This is very important to remember. Eve has the ability to convince The Player to go against what he knows to be right without ever knowing the consequences of the action she is asking him to take. She thinks that if it looks good, it must be good and so she acts.

The Player cannot allow a woman to introduce him to something foreign he knows is bad for him because he will

"With persuasive words she led him astray; she seduced him with her smooth talk; All at once he followed her like an ox going to the slaughter, like a deer stepping into a noose. till and an arrow pierces his liver, like a bird darting into a snare, little knowing it will cost him his life. Now then my sons, listen not me; pay attention to what I say. Do not let your heart turn to her ways or stray into her paths…"

Proverbs 7:21 – 25

be held responsible for the outcome, not her. He must remember that he is the head and the decision maker and must accept the responsibilities of those roles. This comes with the partnership with Eve, being a part of Adam. He will feel the consequences first, and then she will feel them.

"Many are victims she has brought down; her slain are mighty throng. Her house is a highway to the grave, leading to her chambers of death."

Proverbs 7:26 – 27

Eve convinced Adam to take the forbidden fruit and what happened? She was forced to suffer. She had to pay for what she asked Adam to do. Did she ever take this into consideration when she made the decision to eat the fruit? No, she did not. She did not think past the initial pleasure of tasting the fruit. She could not understand the pain that would come with that pleasure. Women cannot see the price of their desires. They cannot see that the problems that plague them are caused by the pleasures they seek. The Player has to recognize that a woman does not know what makes her happy. That is why it is imperative that he knows what will make himself happy so he is not distracted by the fruit of Eve. The pleasure of the fruit is what makes the journey hard.

The Player must be wary of any foreign fruit that a woman introduces. This fruit may be in the form of teachings, drugs, alcohol or her vagina. If a woman strives to teach him a foreign doctrine that does not feel right or that goes against the teachings of his parents, he should not accept it. If a woman introduces a foreign substance for him to take or try, it can lead to a road of difficulty. Drugs are a no-no. If a woman tries to give them to him, The Player should say no with the understanding that the woman does not know what she is doing. When The Player listens to Eve and tries a forbidden fruit, it makes life difficult for the both of them. The fruit will be seductively sweet and appetizing with the appearance of empowerment. There will be those who will warn him not to take it; he should heed their warnings. This fruit can lead to destruction.

Know Thyself

Adam knows better; Eve does not. When Adam says no, Eve listens. Adam imposes his will for Eve to obey. So first and foremost, The Player must know better. He must know what he is saying no to and why. Just the same, if he says yes, he should know what he is saying yes to and why. In order to know what is good and bad for him, it is important that The Player knows himself. When he has advanced to the Phase of Adam, he has learned through research what is good and what is bad for him. He should know what he likes and what he does not like.

"Do the best you can until you know better. Then when you know better, Do better."

Maya Angelou

In addition to knowing himself, The Player should remember that "mother knows best." He should listen to his primary female guardian in the ways of a woman. If his mother tells him not to do something, he should listen. This is the Path of Knowledge and Wisdom.

Finding Eve

In order to win, The Player must find his Eve, the woman that will be his ultimate helper. She should be built "Ford Tough." She should know what it takes to be Eve, have the qualifications, and be able to execute. These are things that The Player should look for when seeking out his Eve. These are attributes that The Player should also possess, or should at least desire to have. This is why it is important to use the Power of the Question, discussed in a later chapter, to learn what attributes are within. Eve will be the other half that brings them to The Player. She will be the source of the love, light and energy needed to make it to the highest levels of The Game. She has to be willing to submit and use her energy and force for the betterment of the team. She has to recognize the plan and be down 100%. This is what The Player looks for when seeking out his Eve.

"Many men are wise about many things and ignorant about themselves"

St. Bernard

Through the process of growing from the Lad Phase to the Adam Phase, The Player will encounter many ladies but only a few of them will possess the qualities of Eve. The Player has to recognize them when he sees them. He has to show her who he is and she has to choose him. Once this happens, he can now access the higher levels of The Game. The Player is the key, and Eve is the door.

Eve has qualities that are built up by Adam, and in turn, she builds Adam up. The Player's Eve should be a reflection of himself. She should reflect his qualities and watch his back. She should never be in front of The Player when it comes to decision making so as not to block his view of what is in front of him.

"He who finds a wife finds what is good and receives favor from the LORD."

Proverbs 18:22 NIV

Picture a mirror and how it reflects the image in front of it. Some mirrors reflect images that are disproportionate, just as some women can bring out the worst in a man. Eve brings a balance, reflecting The Player's best qualities and hiding his worst flaws. She should be able to share his brightness and smooth over his rough edges. He is strong where she is weak, and vice versa. It is like a fantastic duo, each member bringing unique greatness to form a single force. Adam and Eve work together to form and spread the Kingdom of Adam.

Eve's energy and will to create and sustain allows The

Player to go out and spread his light upon the world. The Player uses the fuel from Eve to go out into the world to feed the family. Her willingness to get things done should not be squandered, but targeted. Her light should be shown through her actions and not her mouth (unless her task is to go out and spread the word of the light). Her ambition is a reflection of the inner ambition of The Player. She should reflect his greatness in her own unique way.

In understanding that Eve is Adam's partner and assistant, it is important to re-introduce the importance of knowledge of self. The Player must strive to know his true self. Upon knowing and recognizing his true self, he can recognize his Eve and the power she possesses. Knowledge of self is not only important in recognizing Eve, it is essential in teaching her. It is the key in establishing her role in reaching the goal The Player has set.

The Player offers his Eve his one of a kind plethora of Jewels in the form of his unique knowledge, wisdom and understanding. It will be these Jewels that will attract, keep, and sustain Eve. If The Player is loyal, dedicated and does not believe in quitting, Eve will be the same. She will give these attributes back to him when the world does not. He must demonstrate these things himself and Eve will do

"Two are better than one, because they have a good return for their labor: If either of them falls down, one can help the other up. But pity anyone who falls and has no one to help them up."

Proverbs 4:9 – 10

the same. If The Player wrongs Eve, he wrongs himself. It is essential he treat Eve as his future Queen if he sees himself becoming a King. Bestowing the keys of the Kingdom to Eve will open the door to his dreams.

The Player must recognize the power of his woman. By recognizing the power of his woman, he recognizes the power within himself, a power that can be tapped into and built upon. At the same time, he has the responsibility to be the source of her knowledge, wisdom and understanding. He has to know what to tell Eve to do. He has to know why she should do it, and how it benefits her as well as the team. It is The Player's burden to know the outcome of the actions of his team. He has to know what everyone's role is and how playing their position will result in a win for the team. It is The Player's burden, and his woman is there to help him. Eve and his journal are the two places The Player can go to share his thoughts about his goals, feelings, aspirations, and the world in general. Eve should have understanding. That is her burden.

"No man succeeds without a good woman behind him. Wife or mother, if it is both, he is twice blessed indeed."

Godfrey Winn

If The Player has a dominate personality, he should find a woman who is submissive. If he is passive, he needs a feisty woman. She will bring out the necessary fire and tenacity needed to transcend the levels of The Game. The transmission of the knowledge should not be difficult. The Player should feel comfortable sharing his thoughts with Eve. He should be able to trust her and should never do anything to break this trust. He must govern himself in such a way that his partner does not do him harm. Eve knows Adam's weak spots; The Player does not want to make an enemy out of her. What Adam does to Eve, the Creator will do to Adam.

All in all, Eve should be built to handle the ups and downs, the vices and virtues, the good and the bad of The Player. She should know the obstacles of The Game and be able to face them, mirroring The Player's ambitions. He has to inform Eve that there is no quitting or going back; there is only going forward and up. The difficulty may increase but the view and reward are worth it. The Player cannot quit on Eve, and Eve cannot quit on The Player. He provides for Eve, and Eve sustains him.

"Opposites should not only attract. They should also learn from each other."

Ralph Sarza

Chapter Review

- There was an urge for the Creator to create a partner and companion for Adam, and he formed this being from the rib of Adam. When Adam looked at the creation, he saw himself. He named this creation Eve.
- Eve is the other half of Adam; they are one. They are equal in quality. Adam is the thinking part, and Eve is the doing part. Adam is the head, Eve is the tail. Adam receives light, Eve reflects light. Two of the same, are Adam and Eve.
- Eve can introduce to The Player a foreign object that can make life hard. This foreign object can come in many forms including, teachings, drugs, alcohol, and her vagina. This foreign object is going to make life harder. It will increase the difficulty of challenges. The foreign object can lead to demons, incarceration, day to day problems, and even death.
- It is up to The Player to know better and do better. He has to use the power of knowledge to tell Eve no when she offers a foreign object.
- Eve is Adam's assistant and helper. She helps The Player play The Game of life. She should know her role, her importance and the rewards of winning. She should welcome the challenge and be ready to meet it.
- Eve is a mirror of Adam. She reflects Adam and his greatness. How Adam treats Eve is how the world will treat him. It is through Eve that Adam will become King.
- The Player has to have knowledge of self to clearly recognize Eve and to properly lead her. He has to know himself inside and out. It is the role of The Player to provide knowledge, wisdom, and understanding to Eve.

God created man in His own image, in the image of God He created him; male and female He created them (Genesis 1:27)

Lilith

Unbeknownst to many, there are two creation stories. The previous chapter told the Creation story in which Eve was created from the rib of Adam. There is an earlier creation story that can be found in the first chapter of Genesis in which man and woman were both created in the likeness of the Creator at the same time. In this story, woman was created out of Earth, not from Adam's rib. This woman is not Eve. She was not created to be his helper or assistant but as a separate and equal creature independent of Adam.

Many scholars believe the story of Lilith was inspired by "Lillu," mythical female vampires of the Sumerians, or the Mesopotamian succubae (called "lilin") which were female night demons. Although the Babylonian Talmud references Lilith, it is not until the 9th or 10th century that the character of Lilith is first associated with the story of Creation.

Folly is an unruly woman; she is simple and knows nothing. She sits at the door of her house, on a seat at the highest point of the city, calling out to those who pass by who go straight on their way, "Let all who are simple come to my house!" To those who have no sense she says, "Stolen water is sweet, food eaten in secret is delicious!" But little do they know that the dead are there, that her guests are deep in the realm of the dead." Proverbs 9:13 - 18

This is the story of Lilith, an assertive wife who rebelled against God and husband, was replaced by another woman, and was demonized in Jewish folklore as a dangerous killer of babies, according to the Alphabet of Ben Sira:

Lilith was Adam's first wife but the couple fought all the time. They didn't see eye-to-eye on matters of sex because Adam always wanted to be on top while Lilith also wanted a turn in the dominant sexual position. When they could not agree, Lilith decided to leave Adam. She uttered God's name and flew into the air, leaving Adam alone in the Garden of Eden. God sent three angels after her and commanded them to bring her back to her husband by force if she would not come willingly. But when the angels found her by the Red Sea they were unable to convince her to return and could not force her to obey them. Eventually a strange deal is struck, wherein Lilith promised not to harm newborn children if they are protected by an amulet with the names of the three angels written on it.

Other variations of the story characterize Lilith as a succubus, a beautiful woman and seducer of men. Her offspring were said to be demon children.

"Say to wisdom, "you are my sister, and call insight your intimate friend, that they may keep you from the loose woman, from the adulteress with her smooth words."

Proverbs 7:4 – 5

The Player that is T.W.T.B.H. recognizes the creation of the spirit of Lilith. She is the woman who will not submit to his will and will cause him the most pain and destruction. She has the ability to mislead The Player from the goal and the prize. She seduces him sexually, sucking him dry of energy and resources. She will get him into trouble and will leave him to deal with it by himself. She will talk a great game, but will cause the most pain. In the end, she will not submit and she will leave The Player.

Master Seductress

The first thing The Player must recognize is that Lilith is not a part of him the way Eve is and does not feel the pain he feels. With that being said, neither is she his mirror. She can see destruction in front of The Player and has the ability to lead him right into it. Lilith can intentionally cause destruction to The Player. Afterward, she will tell him he should have known better. The Player should also recognize that he cannot make Lilith submit to his will. He cannot help her. He should not even try. In trying to help Lilith, he will find himself in terrible situations. The Player cannot help Lilith but Lilith can destroy The Player.

Lilith will try to seduce The Player with sex, drugs and power. She can be found in the club, at parties, and in social outings. The Player should be extremely careful when he is out on the town, especially when in a relationship with Eve. A run-in with Lilith has the potential to be very destructive. Lilith is known for breaking the rules. She causes The Player to do little things that he knows are not right in order to be with her. His little devious behavior has the potential to escalate into more serious transgressions in order to impress her. In the end, he finds destruction and an empty hand. The Player cannot have Lilith because she does not want him.

Although The Player must be mindful, he should not worry as long as he heeds certain warning signs. When he encounters a new woman, he should watch for certain characteristics to avoid falling prey to Lilith. Lilith will not listen, and she always has a sad story to tell. The Player should take notice if he only wants to be around a woman when he wants to have sex, or that is all they have in common. Trouble follows Lilith. If being around a woman brings out the negative side in The Player to the point where trouble begins to follow, he should consider this woman to be Lilith. Any woman that asks him to break rules and stray from his path is also Lilith.

The Player can also recognize Lilith by her desire to "go out." She has to go out. The Player should be mindful of the costume she puts on when she does. When she goes out, she is known for "getting turned up." He should be mindful if she likes to go out to drink instead of staying home. This is a recipe for disaster, especially if she does not want to stop. The spirit that inhabits her when she drinks is distinctively different and does not follow the same rules that govern her when she is sober. The power of Lilith is at its most powerful when she has engaged in drinking alcohol. The Player should avoid a woman who has consumed too much alcohol. If he ever questions the sobriety of a woman, he should not go any further. The pleasure is not worth the problems that can follow. A woman who drinks and engages in Lilith-like behavior may be ashamed of this behavior and may blame it on The Player. He will have to fight the battle of his life against a demon he created with Lilith. A demon is an event that comes back to haunt The Player and causes problems for him in The Game.

Demons are Real

Encounters with Lilith have the ability to create demons. These demons will come in the form of events that are negative but feel good in the moment. These events may or may not feel good to Lilith because they are just a means to the ultimate goal – the heartbreak and destruction of the will of Adam. These events will be caused by the negative qualities that Lilith brings out in The Player. She causes him to take a low road that he does not recognize to be extremely hard and leads him to a dead end. It only feels good to the five senses. Lilith is a "freak." She is sexually seductive in nature. She really gets the five senses going, but she comes with a price and that price is not worth paying.

"I noticed among the young men, a youth who lacked judgment. He was going down the street near her corner, walking along in the direction of her house at twilight as the day was fading, as the dark of night set in. Then out came a woman to meet him, dressed like a prostitute and with crafty intent. (She is loud and defiant, her feet never stay at home; now in the street, now in the squares, at every corner she lurks)...

These events cannot be underestimated nor understated. These demons can include the night a man commits a stupid crime to impress a woman; or the night he hit that woman; or worse, the night he had sex with that woman who had too much to drink. Those demons come back to haunt these men. They cost him time, money, stature, and they make life extremely difficult. Having sex with Lilith is a big no-no. If The Player is having sex with a woman he believes to be Lilith, he should stop immediately. He is giving her the energy and life force she needs to destroy him.

"... She took hold of him and kissed and wit a brazen. "I have fellowship offerings at home; today I fulfilled my vows. So I came out to meet you; I looked for you and have found you! I have covered my bed with colored lines from Egypt..."

If a woman is the direct reason for an encounter with the police or she is the reason for The Player going to jail, he needs to leave her alone when he comes out. He is not to answer a phone call or email. Nothing. If a woman allows The Player to go to jail, especially if she is the cause, she has no love for him. The proof is in the pudding. Eve, a woman who loves Adam, would not have The Player purposely incarcerated. Do not pay attention to a lady's word; pay attention to the effects of her actions.

The Player must keep his ears open and use his Eye of Investigation and Observation to assure the avoidance of Lilith. This includes being mindful of situations where Lilith is present. She is known for creating situations where people get set up. The Player must be mindful of who Lilith introduces to him. She is the source of deception and nothing positive or beneficial will come from her. It is all an illusion. She has the ability to get The Player killed, and she will not have any remorse. She will not care. The weaker he appears, the more he pleads and asks why, the more she basks in the glory of victory. Her favorite sayings are "He is a grown man and can make his own decisions," or "I didn't put a gun to his head to make him do it." She will use these lines to explain why The Player should be blamed for an idea that was of her creation. It takes the will of Adam, the Creator and three angels to defeat Lilith, so be mindful of this when challenging her.

"... I have perfumed my bed with myrrh, aloes and cinnamon. Come let's drink deep of love till morning; let's enjoy ourselves with love! My husband is not at home he has gone a long journey. He took his purse filled with money and will not be home till full moon."

Proverbs 7:7 – 20 NIV

Exit Strategy

If Lilith enters The Player's life, people close to him will tell him that she is dangerous. He should listen to them. If the woman is Lilith, she cannot be controlled, she will not submit, and she will cause destruction. It is plain and simple. In the creation of The Game, this is the role she decided to play. She plays the role of the deceiver and destroyer. She deceives The Player and then leads him to destruction through his own actions. The Player needs to heed this warning before interacting with Lilith because once engaged with one, he has to be very careful. If he hurts Lilith, she will make it a point to destroy him. He can only outthink her by creating a situation in which she removes herself. And once she is gone, he must never allow her to come back.

If The Player is already engaged with Lilith, he has a lot of work to do. He has to run her away with the light and not allow her to come back. He has to listen to instruction and surround himself with light. When she threatens to leave, he motivates her to do so. Once an opportunity presents itself to cut off communication with Lilith, The Player should do so. He should not answer her phone calls or emails. If he sees her in public, he should run from her. It is better to run from Lilith than to make her mad and try to fight her. She is a foe that can suck up all of The Player's resources in war.

If The Player maintains his proper path, he can avoid Lilith. She is a distraction and, if he has knowledge of self, The Player will see her as such. Warning bells will ring from all directions. If he listens, he can bypass the problems of Lilith. By keeping an eye on his tongue and his little head, The Player can avoid creating demons that he will have to pay for later. He will be mindful of what Lilith is, avoid her, and, consequently, escape all the deviant behavior and correction that comes with her.

"Like a gold ring in a pig's snout is a beautiful woman who shows no discretion."

Proverbs 11:22 **NIV**

Chapter Review

- There was a creation story before Eve. This story included the creation of a woman who was made of Earth and in the likeness of the Creator, just like Adam. She was created independently of Adam, unlike Eve, who was created from Adam. Her name is Lilith.
- Lilith is a woman who will not submit to the will of Adam. She will deceive The Player and eventually destroy his will. She is very seducing to the five senses and causes The Player to engage in devious behavior
- The devious behavior that The Player engages in through Lilith will create demons that will come back to haunt him. They can plague The Player for a lifetime if he is not careful.
- Lilith is most powerful when she has been drinking and wants to be social. It is when a woman is under the influence of alcohol that Lilith can do the most damage. THE PLAYER IS NOT TO HAVE SEX WITH ANY WOMAN WHO HE QUESTIONS MAY HAVE HAD TOO MUCH TO DRINK. If there is ever a question of her sobriety, there is no sex or intimacy at all. It is not worth it.
- The Player should take heed of the warnings from loved ones and those who know her. If they say she is trouble, she is trouble, and there is nothing anyone can do about it. By interacting with her, The Player is inviting trouble into his life.
- If in a current relationship with Lilith, The Player must create a door for her to leave and never let her back in. If Adam is having sex with Lilith, he is to discontinue immediately and look for a way to cut off communication with her without making her mad.

- The Player can avoid Lilith and her traps by having proper knowledge of self and using it to be aware of her. Also, he should keep his focus on the Big Head and The Game so he will not be easily sidetracked. He should avoid her stomping grounds which are the late night bars, clubs and concerts.

The LORD said to her "Two nations are in your womb,
and two peoples from within you will be separated;
one people will be stronger than the other,
and the older will serve the younger."

When the time came for her to give birth, there were twin boys in her womb. The first to come out was red, and his whole body was like a hairy garment; so they named him Esau. After this, his brother came out, with his hand grasping Esau's heel; so he was named Jacob. Isaac was sixty years old when Rebekah gave birth to them.

The boys grew up, and Esau became a skillful hunter, a man of the open country, while Jacob was content to stay at home among the tents. Isaac, who had a taste for wild game, loved Esau, but Rebekah loved Jacob.

Once when Jacob was cooking some stew, Esau came in from the open country, famished. He said to Jacob, "Quick, let me have some of that red stew! I'm famished!"

...

Jacob replied, "First sell me your birthright."

"Look, I am about to die," Esau said. "What good is the birthright to me?"

"There is no pride like the pride of ancestry."

Benjamin Disraeli

But Jacob said, "Swear to me first." So he swore an oath to him, selling his birthright to Jacob.

Then Jacob gave Esau some bread and some lentil stew. He ate and drank, and then got up and left.

Battle Esau

In the story of Esau and Jacob, there is a confrontation that can be found within every young black lad – the battle of the birthright. A birthright is defined as a right, privilege, or possession to which a person is entitled by birth. Esau, the hunter, finds himself hungry and goes to his younger twin brother Jacob, the farmer, for help. Jacob convinces his brother to sell his birthright, which leads Jacob to becoming Israel the King. These characters represent stages within The Player. Esau the Hunter is the Lad Phase of The Game, Jacob the Farmer is the Adam Phase, and Israel is the King Phase.

Esau the Hunter represents the physical nature of The Player. Esau lives and dies for the moment. A hunter uses his physical ability to impose his will upon nature. If a hunter does not find success on the hunt, he starves. If a hunter is hurt and cannot hunt, he finds it extremely difficult to eat. The hunter relies on his body and his instinct

"When I was a boy in my father's house, still tender and only a child of my mother, he taught me and said, " Lay hold of my words will all your heart; keep my commands and you will live. Get wisdom, get understanding; do not forget my words or swerve from them. Do not forsake wisdom, and she will protect you; love her, and she will watch over you."

Proverbs 4:3 – 6 NIV

to out think an animal. Sometimes he wins. Sometimes he loses.

In this story, Esau has failed on his hunt and he is hungry. This represents the Lad Phase of The Game. It is The Player's physical nature, the fulfilling of the desires of the body. The Player in the Lad Phase tends to rely on instinct and defines himself by his physical attributes. He goes out in the world and uses his body to experience it. He learns his favorite foods, cars, places and experiences. This is also the stage in which The Player begins to seek out Eve.

Although the hunter instinct is valuable, even necessary, playing The Game solely on the physical level will only get The Player so far. This is the equivalent of playing the greatest video game without reading any material, just picking up the remote and playing. It is equivalent to playing Madden, 007, Zelda, Call of Duty, Grand Theft Auto, Mario or the Final Fantasy series without ever picking up a book or reading a blog. The challenge of figuring out such games may be fun, but it would also be extremely time consuming, involve a whole lot of trial and error, and result in multiple failures. It is the same playing The Game as Esau. Esau picks up his weapon and relies on his instinct to win. And in the story of Jacob and Esau, he lost. A loss in The Game could be devastating, even fatal.

"Without self-knowledge, without understanding the working and functions of his machine, man cannot be free, he cannot govern himself and he will always remain a slave."

George Gurdjieff

This mentality can be seen when a man seeks out things for a moment's pleasure without looking at the long-term cost. When a man makes a decision for instant gratification without consideration of the consequences, he is exhibiting his Esau nature. For example, a man that gets drunk and cheats on his woman with a woman who simply looks good is operating in his Esau nature. So is the one who sells drugs or steals just for the momentary gratification. There is no consideration for the consequences in any of these actions. The physical pleasure of a sexy woman and the fast cash of drug dealing or robbery last but for a moment. The loss of a good woman, unwanted pregnancy, sexually transmitted diseases, jail time and a criminal record have long-lasting effects that are detrimental. Even so, men will make these decisions, under the influence of Esau, and end up down and out, begging for something to eat.

"He is not wise that is not wise for himself."

Aristotle

One of the greatest Jewels contained within the story of Jacob and Esau is revealed when Jacob, Esau's twin, asks his brother to sell his birthright in exchange for the lentil soup. The truth is, it is a gift to be born a black man. The Player's greatness comes in his birth and his recognition of self. He must recognize that the black man is the Creator's first born and he has the potential to be King. But he can also be misled into selling his birthright to the throne.

Esau selling his birthright to Jacob represents the moment when The Player ceases to live in the moment and begins to live with purpose. He begins to govern himself as if he wants to be somebody, somebody like a King. He begins to respect himself and others. He becomes in tune with nature instead of being afraid of it and trying to conquer it. When The Player takes the knowledge of self and apply it with the intention to grow and become a King, he is transitioning from the Lad Phase to the Adam Phase.

"He who brings trouble on his family will inherit only wind and the fool will be servant to the wise."

Proverbs 11:29 NIV

Essentially, this story represents The Player's desire for a better way to play The Game. It can be compared to an athlete that plays The Game on instinct versus one who grows through practice and coaching. Instinct will only get The Player so far. When Esau sells his birthright for food, he is giving up the right to do it his way and is giving in to the will of his brother, Jacob the Farmer.

When The Player has taken on the nature of Jacob the Farmer, he has ascended to the Adam Phase of The Game. It is in this stage that The Player begins to use what it is he knows in order to win. The Lad Phase was all about learning his animal nature. The Adam Phase is where he begins to use his brain. It is the stage in which The Player puts his own spin on the things he learned through his experiences in the world and starts putting them to good use.

Jacob the Farmer has mastered the land. In mastering the land, he has learned planning, patience, and saving. He understands the concept of planting the seed now and reaping the reward later. He has the patience to wait. Jacob has mastered his nature instead of battling it. Esau has to hunt wild animals, which sometimes elude him, whereas Jacob has mastered the Earth from which he was created. He reaches into the same Earth and is able to feed himself and his family. In mastering the land, Jacob masters himself and puts himself in position to win the ultimate goal, which is the birthright. Jacob wants to live for tomorrow instead of worrying about today. He wants to sustain now and plan for tomorrow so that can he can rule forever.

"In mastery there is bondage, in bondage there is mastery."

Cicero

The battle between Esau and Jacob, hunter nature versus farmer nature, plays out within every black man. This causes a dissonance. One part of him wants everything in front of him at that moment, and another part of him wants to plan and act for the future. And so there is an internal strife.

In order to play The Game like Jacob, The Player must

T.W.T.B.H., utilizing the blueprint of how Jacob would do things. The Player just has to practice the blueprint to curve and fine-tune his animal nature to win. This process is understood in how The Player conducts himself and where he plants his seed. This means The Player starts T.W.T.B.H. in order to find fertile ground, and then uses his Esau nature to plant his seed, and his Jacob nature to harvest the rewards.

To make the transition from Esau to Jacob, hunter to farmer, The Player has to move beyond finding the quick and easy way. Joy comes in the journey. Anything instantly received can be instantly lost. Jacob governs himself in a manner now so he can win later. The Player has to learn to govern himself in every moment so that he can win in the future. Remember that the Creator told Adam that he would have to work hard to toil the land. This means that road to greatness is going to be difficult no matter what Adam does. Jacob has mastered the journey to capture what belongs to him, the birthright of the firstborn, and the ability to be the next King.

"Better to master one, than engage 10."

Thomas Fuller

The point of this story is that Esau and Jacob are within The Player. They are the two paths of play that he can choose. He can choose to play by instinct, and deal with life on a situation by situation basis; or, he can play by planning his plays according to the rules, instructions and correction. In order to be successful, The Player must learn to master his ability based on the fundamentals. Esau free-styles, plays street ball, is a jack of all trades and a master of none. Jacob masters the fundamentals in his own unique way, is playing on the highest of levels, and is known as the great one.

To make it clear and simple: Esau acts and then learns; Jacob learns and then acts. In order to T.W.T.B.H., The Player must understand The Game and then put forth the effort. The first step in predicting and understanding reactions and consequences is understanding the initial actions. The Player must always be aware of what he is doing and why he is doing it. He is always aware of the consequences and is prepared for them. He always strives to know his intent, the "why" behind his actions. If The Player asks himself why he is doing something, he will be motivated to learn and grow in The Game.

"Whoever loves discipline loves knowledge, but he who hates correction is stupid."

Proverbs 12:1 NIV

All of this is tied into how Adam interacts with Eve. Adam understands that life is more than the moment, and sex is creation. It is time to take a moment to discuss what it means to have sex. Sex between a man and a woman in-

"

volves the man inserting his penis into a woman, culminating in the ejaculation of his God's Power into her womb. This one singular act can bring forth into The Player's life an angel or a demon. This is why it is very important for The Player to recognize the power of the Little Head. The Little Head has the power to bring forth life into the physical world, a being made directly from its creator, and it has the potential to be a blessing or a curse.

"Perfection of hearing is not hearing others but oneself. Perfection of vision is not seeing others but oneself."

Chaung Tzu

The key here is to understand that **SEX CREATES.** Plain and simple. This creation can come in many forms. The most obvious is a child. Sex creates life in the form of children. It also creates in the form of bonds. Sex creates relationships. Sex creates health issues. Sex creates life and death scenarios. Sex in certain forms is illegal and creates problems with the law. Sex has the ability to send a man to jail.

Esau only sees the pleasure of the figure; Jacob sees the consequence. Esau uses his ability to hunt; Jacob uses his ability to find fertile ground. One looks outside himself; the other looks within himself. Esau looks to have sex anytime with whomever looks good at the time; Jacob looks for the right woman and the right time. One looks for the pleasure of the moment; the other wants the pleasure of the experience. Esau understands that once the meat is done, he has to find more, and so he is constantly hunting. Jacob, on the other hand, finds his land, does his thing and lets his food grow. He does not have to spend the energy chasing a moment because he is living an experience.

These are two distinct levels in The Game. Esau plays The Game for the moment and Jacob plays The Game for the experience. Esau plays The Game out of urge, and Jacob plays The Game for purpose. This can be seen in how The Player chooses his Eve. Does he choose a woman who can give him satisfaction for the moment or for a lifetime? Esau looks at a woman in the present and sees only that which she can give him now. Jacob determines what a woman can do for his future and plants his seed in fertile ground.

"He who ignores discipline despises himself, but whoever heeds correction gains under-standing."

Proverbs 15:32 NIV

In order to T.W.T.B.H., The Player must begin to learn himself, his environment, and his goal so he can find the right woman to help him win The Game. A successful player, one who is exhibiting the nature of Jacob, learns his woman and waits for the right time to plant his seed. He understands patience and the importance of timing when it comes to planting his seed because he is a farmer.

In either the Lad Phase or the Adam Phase, The Player

must be mindful of the women he is around, as well as in whom, when and why he plants his seed. His seed is initially his thoughts. Over time it will progress to his physical seed. First comes the planting of thoughts and the creation of a relationship; then comes the planting of the physical seed and the creation of life. This is the process of Jacob.

Wisdom cries out in the street in the squares she raises her voice. At the busiest corner she cries out; at the entrance of the city she speaks: How long, O simple ones, will you love being simple? How long will scoffers delight in their scoffing and fools hate knowledge?

For waywardness kills the simple, and the complacency of fools destroy them

Self-Worth

Life is a thinking man's game and the ability to reach the top is based on The Player's ability to make the right decisions and follow the proper path. The path begins with The Player gaining knowledge, wisdom and understanding. This process is referred to as accumulating Jewels. Accumulating Jewels in The Game builds self-worth in The Player and gives him the power to make the hard decisions that will take him to the next level.

"I [wisdom] walk in the way right-eous-ness, along the paths of choice, be-stowing wealth on those who love me and making treas-uries full."

Proverbs 8:20 – 21 NIV

Why should a woman choose The Player? What would make others want to humble themselves and follow him? What gives The Player the motivation to overcome impossible odds? The answer to these questions is not his car, or his money, or his great athletic ability. It is his knowledge and wisdom. The knowledge The Player has about his car or the understanding he has about the power of his money is the key, not the car or the money itself. This gift may come from his Esau the Hunter nature, but his Jacob the Farmer nature enabled him to use it in an intentional, purposeful, and team way to achieve the ultimate goal. A great athlete who decides to listen to coaching and utilize this coaching in the midst of a game to play at his best for the goal of the overall team is using knowledge and wisdom in conjunction with his ability. The Player transcends The Game when he takes the Jewels he has accumulated and uses his ability to work with them instead of against them.

Jewels can be found everywhere in the day to day world. In order to make a living, people accumulate knowledge and wisdom that will prepare them to do a job that will sustain them in life. People take paths such as school, job corps, or the military to find or further a gift they have to survive in the world. An individual's ability to get a job rests in his knowledge and application of the traits needed for the job. Over the course of an individual's life, he must have made decisions to learn and practice the traits needed for that particular job or there would be no motivation to get it. This acquisition of knowledge and experience is accumulating Jewels. The individual accumulated the Jewels needed to get the job and transcended levels when he used them to further himself. The Jewels he accumulates

"Do not set foot on the path of the wicked or walk in the way of evil men or walk in the way of evil men. Avoid it, do not travel on it; turn from it and go on your way."

Proverbs 4:14 – 15 NIV

and his ability and desire to share them allow The Player to walk through portals that will take him to higher levels of The Game. Knowledge and wisdom are essential to growth.

To do well in The Game, The Player must gain knowledge of himself, how he functions and how to master his Esau Nature. In doing so, he has made the decision to better himself and opportunities will make themselves available to him. Opportunities to change his surroundings, his fortune and his level status come with The Player taking the time to learn about himself and practicing to better himself. Once The Player makes the decision to become a student of The Game instead of just a player, he has taken the first step to mastering it.

Learning comes in all different forms. It comes from reading, listening to audiobooks, watching documentaries, and the best teacher of them all – life. If The Player takes time to learn from those he encounters on a day to day basis, he will learn and grow a lot faster. Once he decides to make every minute of his life a learning experience, he steps onto the right path, the Path of Knowledge, Wisdom and Understanding. With the mind-state that he can learn twenty-four-seven from the people around him and his

"By me [wisdom] kings reign and rulers issue decrees that are just; by me princes govern, and nobles—all who rule on earth. I love those who love me, and those who seek me find me. With me are riches and honor, enduring wealth and prosperity. My fruit is better than fine gold; what I yield surpasses choice silver."

Proverbs 8:15 – 19 NIV

journal as a place to log the Jewels he accumulates, The Player can move without stumbling and falling. Taking the time to learn from those around him, The Player can familiarize himself with his surroundings and discover the best path to be successful on his journey through The Game.

What The Player knows and what The Player does will directly affect his ability to attract Eve. When The Player realizes who he is and what his purpose is, he can then attract a mate that can help him achieve this mission. His knowledge and ability to get things done will entice women. It is up to The Player to use his knowledge and wisdom to find his Eve out of the pack of women who will be attracted to him. As discussed earlier, all women are not Eves. And not all Eves are meant for a particular Player. The Player wants the right Eve for him, the Eve that brings out his best qualities and is strong in the areas that he is weak. The Player must have the knowledge of himself first and foremost. The Player decides who he is, not Eve. If Eve decides who The Player is, he will be a loser, and a miserable one. The Player must see the King within himself first.

"Who knows himself knows others; for heart can be compared with heart."

Chinese Proverb

By accumulating Jewels, The Player's self-worth will

grow. He will have the strength and confidence to make the tough decisions because he possesses the power of knowledge. He will know better and therefore do better, because he understands what the outcome will be and he knows where he wants to go. Knowledge, wisdom and understanding are extremely empowering. With the accumulation of each, The Player grows in power. He grows in his ability to function, play and win. He learns what to do, when to do it, and how to do it in his own unique way. All this gives him confidence.

As The Player practices his knowledge, wisdom and understanding, he will begin to feel what it is like to experience the King Phase. He will feel the sensation of creating his own reality and the enjoyment of making the right decisions. He will have understanding of the difficult times and possess the motivation to overcome them. He will also have the humbleness to appreciate the mountaintop view. The Player will have awareness of where he is in The Game and the role he has to play. He will not feel lost.

Now fully aware of the power of knowledge and wisdom, The Player is ready to go out and play The Game. He knows that he has the power of the Creator within

I undertook great projects: I built houses for myself and planted vineyards. I made gardens and parks and planted all kinds of fruit trees in them. I made reservoirs to water groves of flourishing trees. I bought male and female slaves as well—the delights of a man's heart. I amassed silver and gold for myself, and the treasure of kings and provinces... I became greater by far than anyone in Jerusalem before me. In all this my wisdom stayed with me.
Ecclesiastes 2::4 – 9

him. He knows and understands that he has the ability to create angels and demons for himself. He understands the necessity to learn about himself and master his nature to become a King. He understands that this is a team game, and that he must train to be the best leader for his team. It is through his team play that he ultimately feels the King Phase of The Game. The most important piece of understanding for The Player to possess is that he is the creator of his own life and that he is ultimately responsible for it. Without responsibility, there cannot be any successful game play. The Player recognizes that he is Israel, the leader and ruler of his family and Kingdom, and it is his responsibility to know better and to do better so that he can lead them. The process is ongoing and ever present.

The Devil Is a Lie

Life is full of choices and consequences. Who do people accredit their present situations to? Do they recognize that they are the makers of their own reality? The Player creates the things in front of him and it is up to him to figure out how to deal with them in a manner that leads him to success. First, he must recognize that he is the master of his reality and that there are consequences to his actions. He sets the standard and there are ramifications for not meeting that standard or not governing himself accordingly. There are always rules and loopholes. How The Player follows those rules and utilizes the loopholes will dictate the quality of his character.

"Patience and time accomplish more than strength, or anger."

La Fontaine

This seems easy enough. All The Player has to do is simply own up to what he has to do or what he has done. Just think about that for a second. That means taking responsibility for his actions and the situation he is currently in and this is not always easy. People tend to blame others for how they themselves act or for the situation they have found themselves in when in fact it is the Little Head and its warped perception of reality that is at fault.

Take for instance a man that hits his woman. Whose fault

is it that he hit her? Is it her fault for doing something disrespectful, or is it his fault for choosing to use that method of correction? Regardless of the verbal argument that took place before or after, who is ultimately responsible for using violence as a method of correction? To avoid this situation in the future, the man must determine what caused him to hit the woman, what caused him to get so upset he felt the need to put his hands on her. Why did he lose his cool? An effective Player looks to solve whatever is inside himself that pushed him over the limit. He needs to reflect on the behavior that lead him up to that point. Was there a moment he could have stopped and walked away? Why didn't he? What really made him mad? The Player should ask himself these questions and work to fix his own behavior before addressing the woman's.

Sometimes, another person's actions can negatively affect The Player, slowing down or even halting progress. For example, if The Player has a teammate that is having a personal dispute that does not involve The Player but the teammate tries to include The Player in the situation, The Player should be cautious about running and interfering in problems that are not his own. Unnecessary correction may be the result. If The Player has a problem with another person and the problem truly appears to lie within the other

"Too much circulation makes the price go down: The more you are seen and heard from, the more common you appear. If you are already established in a group, temporary withdrawal from it will make you more talked about, even more admired. You must learn when to leave. Create value."

Robert Greene 48 Laws of Power

person, The Player should use the power of absence to address the issue.

The general key to unlocking any problem The Player faces is realizing that the key is within him. When he stops blaming others for his current situation, he takes control of his life and overcomes any sense of helplessness. By learning how to control himself, The Player can learn to control his advisory or problem. The key is acknowledging a problem or situation, admitting that it is of his own making, and then looking within himself for the answer. Looking within oneself is simply determining what role in the solution he plays, then standing up and doing what needs to be done. If The Player is unable to see a solution on his own, and needs to look outside himself by asking others for answers, that is acceptable. The Player is still acknowledging the problem and recognizes that he needs help.

It is important that The Player understands that the devil is a lie. This means ignoring that voice inside that wants to blame everyone else. Doing so will enable The Player to take control of situations because he will look at fixing himself before trying to fix anything else.

The Governor's Favorite Sayings

Catch more flies with honey than shit: You can attract flies with shit. We know flies like shit and will come. But what is shit. Stinking disgusting fecal matter. It is also needed for growth, for it is a representation of cleansing and rebirth; it is what makes the grass grow. Honey on the other hand, is a sweet pleasant sap that is produced from the sweetest of trees. The goodness and sweetness grows in such abundance on the inside that it comes out the pores of the tree. Do you want to attract people with the goodness and sweetness of yourself or the shitty side?

Persistence Overcomes Resistance: It is just as it says. If you keep trying then you will figure out a way to get it done. It's all about the effort and the persistence of it. In The Game, WINNERS NEVER QUIT AND QUITTERS NEVER WIN. This is your world and you are the squirrel and if you look around you'll find whatever nut you are looking for. I cannot stress this enough if you just see what's going on around and put effort, you can achieve everything that you seek. It is all about how you choose to go about achieving the goals that you set forth for yourself. Will you persist down the road of the least resistance for the instant gratifications or embrace the challenges of life and fight the good battle, and win on the highest of levels?

Some things just can't be changed: There are some things about yourself that you cannot change. Whatever this is, it is up to you explain it to people and not allow them to make assumptions. It is best to let them know that it is something that cannot be changed so there is no need to waste time in trying to change it or to even look for a compromise because there is no change. Let me give you an example. If there is a man and a woman in a relationship where the man is lactose intolerant, and his girl loves whole milk and suggests that they drink 2% milk, he can't compromise because it is still going to mess up his stomach. So in that situation there is no need to make the effort.

Everything that Glitters ain't Gold: We live in a time where everything is about looks. A person must understand that everything that looks good is not good. You must use your Eye of Investigation to see how things are and not how they appear to be. Be wary of people who put all their energy into looking good instead of being good.

Grass isn't always greener on the other side: This saying is usually used in a situation where cheating has taken place. A woman may say that a man thought the grass was greener on the other side, meaning what the other woman had to offer was better than what his current lady was offering. A person has to be careful because the grass does appear to be greener on the other side, and there is chance that it is, but when crossing over, there is a chance for an adverse reaction. This situation can be uglier than the previous situation. And depending upon the level you are playing on, this other side that appears to be greener, is most likely a distraction from the goal that is ahead.

Same thing that'll make you laugh will make you cry: This means that the same thing that brings you joy can bring pain. The same thing that brings good times, can bring equal amounts of bad times.

Section 3: Play Time

The previous section discussed the creation of The Player. He was created from Earth in the likeness of the Creator and has been given the chance to play The Game, an opportunity to master himself and become a King of his world. This goal can only be accomplished through teamwork. This section goes into the practices The Player needs to put into place to play The Game and to attract the right teammates.

"The world as we have created it is a process of our thinking. It cannot be changed without changing our thinking."

Albert Einstein

Play Time outlines the day to day practices The Player will need to do to enhance and master his nature. These practices are the keys that will unlock the doors of potential within The Player as well as provide him with the methods of sharing this potential. The Play Time methods are designed to help The Player accumulate Jewels. With the accumulation of the Jewels and the motivation and support of Eve, The Player will be prepared to play The Game on the Adam Phase.

The practices of Play Time will bring forth opportunities to The Player. It is up to him to see them and act upon them. The initial application of the teachings may be difficult; it may seem awkward or opposite to The Player's normal behavior. In such instances, The Player has been doing things backwards. For example, if The Player has been learning from experience, he needs to start using the Power of a Question to learn from another individual's experience. There is a wise saying from Otto Von Bismark that summarizes this point: "Only a fool learns from his own mistakes. The wise man learns from the mistakes of others." By simply inquiring, The Player can accumulate valuable Jewels. When he learns how to use the Power of a Question, The Player can gain the Jewels needed to unlock levels without having to tread the difficult journey or side paths himself. The trail has already been blazed before him.

The daily practice of Play Time should become second nature to The Player. The Key is Me is a set of push-ups The Player does to strengthen his character. Every day, he plans for his future and acts upon these plans regardless of his current Level. He knows that he is meant to be a King, and he will not settle.

The Player should know and understand what he gains from each lesson and how it will help him if he practices it. He will begin to define his inner-self. From there he will learn how to share this inner-self to further his game play.

As for application, Play Time is The Player's work out plan. He should use his journal to write down his accomplishments through the practice of Play Time. In fact, the practice of Play Time should be the source of his journal entries, especially in the beginning. This will give The Player a starting point to look back on as a measurement of growth. As The Player continues to accumulate Jewels in The Game, so should his pen ink grow upon the pages of his journal.

The sections leading up to this point have dealt with The Game structure and environment and the development of The Player. Play Time is where The Player starts playing The Game. He can use this section to begin learning his nature, going out and experiencing the world with these teachings as protection. The Player can feel comfortable engaging in school, athletics, the work world, or the military; or chasing a dream so long as he follows the teachings outlined in Play Time. He will be mentally, as well as morally prepared for the challenges that await him. When The Player has the knowledge of self and is consistently practicing the Play Time techniques, he is effectively T.W.T.B.H. and has the power to make the right decisions to stay on the winning path.

"The teaching of the wise is a fountain of life, turning a man from the snares of the death. Good understanding wins favor, but the way of the faithful is hard."

Proverbs 13:14

Key Is Me

"I'm not a rapper I'm a hustler, I just know how to rap." Jay-Z

Since his introduction to the world in 1996 with his debut album Reasonable Doubt, Jay-Z claimed that he was not a rapper. Even after the success of eleven number one albums, he still says it is his ability to make money that has made him successful, not his lyrical prowess. This is important because he has shown and proved to the world through his actions that he truly is a business man who can rap, not a rapper pretending to be a hustler. He did not let the world define him; he defined himself. He defined who he was and what his future would be and did not allow his success in the world dictate who he was or his course of action. The same should be true for The Player. Knowing his true self and keeping it in mind throughout the play of The Game is the key to his success.

Take for example, a student-athlete. A student athlete is a student first and foremost. He uses his ability to further himself in the learning process so he will be better prepared for The Game, not just his athletic game. The student is at school to learn and this must be the focal point because it is what will sustain the athlete after The Game. The glory of The Game is exciting and intoxicating but the

"Whoever loves money never has enough; whoever loves wealth is never satisfied with their income. This too is meaningless. As goods increase, so do those who consume them. And what benefit are they to the owners except to feast their eyes on them?"

Ecclesiastes 5:10 – 11 NIV

athlete cannot lose sight of the fact that he is a student first. A dedicated student is prepared to sacrifice the fun life now to enjoy being a King later. If the student-athlete recognizes this, he will be a better athlete, will be better in life after graduation, and will transcend to levels of Kingship that the athlete who puts sports first will fail to achieve. Why does this happen? Athletes that know how to study and use knowledge will be better prepared mentally for the stress of The Game. They will have the knowledge, wisdom and dedication to make better decisions. They will have a better understanding of how sacrificing themselves can benefit the team.

"I have seen something else under the sun: The race is not to the swift or the battle to the strong, nor does food come to the wise or wealth to the brilliant or favor to the learned; but time and chance happen to them all."

Ecclesiastes 9:11 NIV

The Player that understands that he is a student of life, understands that his ability to be a success in his endeavors rests on his ability to be a successful student. If he cannot recognize his role as student, there is little opportunity to be anything else. If there is an opportunity, it will have a hard learning curve and will be difficult. If The Player practices being a good student, it will manifest itself in his other abilities just as Jay-Z's ability to make money made his ability to be a successful rapper a lot easier.

The Player's ability to learn about himself enables him to use Esau to entice Jacob. If The Player does what he does best, opportunity will present itself to him. If he practices good judgment by using his Jewels, he can take advantage of these opportunities to transcend to upper realms of The Game. The Game will throw curve balls at The Player, situations that he will have to work through to get to the top. He has to keep in mind who he is and what his goals are to avoid becoming distracted. He cannot get sidetracked by the successes or the trials of the journey. These are part of becoming a King. The journey starts at the bottom and as The Player travels to the top, he will see beautiful places that he will want to stop and enjoy. In doing so he must overcome the urge to become complacent. He must reach his goal. If he does not accomplish what he set out to achieve, either by quitting or settling for less, he will lose and become depressed. He will take these feelings out on his family and his team.

"All hard work brings a profit, but mere talk leads only to poverty."

Proverbs 14:23 NIV

The Player must understand that he has to pay dues to The Game. In other words, he must give himself to The Game. In return, he will find the rewards he seeks. This means putting in work. The Game only pays back The Player after he has put in the work. Regardless of the task, The Player has to keep in mind he is King and it is his responsibility to get the job done. Being King also means always governing himself accordingly. Throughout the process of

The Game, The Player must prove to the world that he is worthy of being King. To accomplish this, he must govern himself in the moment. Whether he is sweeping the streets of his land or being served grapes by nymphs, The Player needs to be aware of the present and planning for the future.

There will be times in which The Player will find himself in difficult situations. These situations should be viewed as tests of character. How The Player chooses to deal with these situations will be a testament to his character. During a civil rights march planned by Martin Luther King, Jr., several young black kids were attacked by dogs and arrested by the Birmingham, Alabama police. While incarcerated, King spoke to the children's parents, saying, "Being in jail is a great time to catch up on reading. Every time I go to jail, I use it as an opportunity to catch up on my reading. If they need books, we will get them books to read." As this example shows, the opportunity to read and better oneself, to triumph over adversity with nobility, exists even in the toughest circumstances.

"A man is praised according to his wisdom, but men with warped minds are despised."

Proverbs 12:8 NIV

Even history's greatest minds required knowledge to make the hard decisions. They faced the same obstacles that The Player faces today. They faced jail, they faced force, they faced difficulty for different reasons. But there is a higher reasoning, a higher purpose that comes from within and it is the same now as it was then. It comes from the Jewels. In jail or in the pulpit, on the rap stage or behind the computer, scoring the winning touchdown or in the face of a great loss, The Player must keep in mind that he is destined to be King. From the bottom to the top, he must recognize where he is going as well as when he will reach the goal. That is when the creation of the Kingdom begins. As goals are reached, the opportunities to create the Kingdom will present themselves. As the number one albums racked up for Jay-Z, so did the opportunities to be the best business man possible. These opportunities formed his kingdom which includes sports, music, spirits, and the arts. He has been able to achieve these things because he never forgot who he was and used every opportunity to showcase himself.

"The wealth of the wise is their crown, but the folly of fools yields folly."

Proverbs 14:24 NIV

When The Player plays The Game, he takes on many roles. In doing so, he must keep in mind what the goal is. The Player knows who he is, so regardless of what the world may say, he knows better. Knowledge of self will not only be useful, but will also be comforting. Knowledge of self will give The Player direction and motivation to find a way to do better and then follow through.

It is important for The Player to see his greatness and believe in his ability to become King, for he will be tested. It is through studying and practicing that The Player will be prepared for these tests. When The Player faces a mountain of disbelievers, he will have the inner knowledge to know better, the strength to keep fighting, to keep playing The Game.

Take for example a young man that works at McDonalds. Working at McDonalds is one of the most common jobs and it is the perfect starting point for a young Player. He is in a situation where all he can do is go up and it is up to him to do so. While flipping burgers, he can either dwell on his current situation or be focused on planning on the future. When not at work, he can use that time to have fun or he can use that time to put in work playing The Game. He can use that time to learn something about his gift, who he is, opening doors to a higher level of The Game. This is the time where putting in work comes into play. Working at McDonalds, The Player is toiling the ground. Studying and playing The Game in his free time, The Player is making a claim to his kingdom. The work that he puts in during his free time will pay off just like the work he does at McDonalds pays off. McDonalds pays now while the studying and acquiring of Jewels pays off later.

"The sleep of a laborer is sweet, whether they eat little or much, but as for the rich, their abundance permits them no sleep."

Ecclesiastes 5:12

In addition to the belief in himself, The Player needs to consider the reflection of Eve. Eve should reflect his greatness. If The Player works at McDonalds but sees himself as a great scholar on the come-up, she should see the same. However The Player sees himself, Eve should show him that same reflection. She should give him the power to overcome any present role he faces, enabling him to reach the next level. In order for this to happen, The Player must show Eve the direction in which he knows he is destined to go. Eve follows The Player and governs herself according to the Jewels he gives her. It is through him that she becomes a Queen and the mother of little princes and princesses. While The Player is working at McDonalds, she is sustained in the fact that he has a plan and the ability to take them to the next level.

Eve is The Player's teammate and is willing to help him in any way possible along the journey. He should look to her for assistance and not be too prideful to accept it. Eve is part of The Player. She should not introduce him to anything new but remind him of a quality that he has forgotten. She will make moves for The Player while he works hard at McDonalds.

"Dishonest money dwindles away, but he who gathers money little by little makes it grow."

Proverbs 13:11 NIV

Chapter Review

- Game play begins when The Player recognizes the goal or the end. Once The Player realizes who he is, he begins the journey of sharing this gift with the world.
- Jewels are knowledge, wisdom and understanding. They have more value than silver and choice gold, and more precious than rubies.
- Jewels are accumulated in the process of The Game and they will unlock doors for The Player to reach the goal or the end. How he uses these Jewels will directly affect his game play and his attraction to Eve.
- Everything begins with the recognition of self, which leads to the application of self, and then the spreading of self. The more knowledge, wisdom and understanding The Player has, better the process becomes, the more efficient and effective The Player, and the more appreciation he has for himself, The Game and his decision making.
- Knowledge of self will bring clarity to the journey and will give it perspective. The Player knows that he has to put in work, and knowledge of self plus planning allows putting in the work to be purposeful. It will become a spring board to the next level instead of a hindrance. While "flipping burgers," The Player is planning, studying and practicing his gift in his free time.
- Eve will be a reflection of the greatness of The Player. No matter the situation, she will bring out the greatness in him because he first knows it himself. She gives him that needed reassurance to put forth the extra effort needed to reach the next level. She is supposed to do all that she can to bring out this inner being that may be hidden by the current level.

"Stand for something or fall for anything."

Base Runner

If The Player is T.W.T.B.H., he is in control of the Little Head. The world of the Little Head is the world of the five senses. It is the world The Player sees with his eyes, tastes with his tongue, the aromas he encounters, the words and sounds he hears, and the sensations of touch. This world is the playing field of The Game.

The number one driving force in the physical world is sex. Sex is one of the physical urges The Player has that can bring him pleasure and utterly destroy him at the same time. Who The Player chooses to have sex with will dictate whether The Player is winning or losing in The Game. Sex with Eve creates positive energy and life in the form of good times and winning. Sex with anything else will create problems, demons and negative challenges. There is no getting around creation through sexual penetration. Even if The Player has sex with a condom, there will be a creation of attachment that will lead to either good times or hard times.

There are a few important things The Player needs to understand about sex:

1. Sex is not free. It can cost The Player his life.

Social Interaction-The process by which we act and react to those around us: Day to day routines with almost constant interactions with others, gives structure and form to what we do; we can learn a great deal about ourselves as social creatures.

Introducing Communication Theory Analysis and Application

2. If The Player "fucks" her, he should be prepared to be "fucked" by her.
3. Sex creates, period.

The moment The Player encounters a woman, The Game is on. Playing by the rules outlined in the Base Runner method enables The Player to transcend levels and create a kingdom and legacy. The Player uses his mind and body as tools to get from point A to point B. To transcend from Lad to Adam and Adam to King, The Player practices self-control to make the right decisions.

As stated earlier, sexual penetration creates life. Sexual penetration has the ability to birth commitment, personal obligation, and emotions. It is commonly understood that sex can create life in the sense of a baby or babies, but what is not commonly known is that it also has the ability to create demons. A demon in this sense is not a scary being from "hell" or the child of the devil. In this instance, a demon is an event that haunts The Player. This means that the sexual act can become something that The Player regrets and has to pay for. This payment may come in the form of child support, a court case, or an unwanted problematic partner. These payments are forms of harsh punishment, and deviations that The Player will have to endure.

"People will calculate the costs and rewards of a given situation and guide their behaviors accordingly. This also includes the possibility that faced w/no rewarding choice, people will choose the least costly alternative. Thus rationalizing provides a fabricated attempt to make a choice look rational after the fact."

Introducing Communication Theory Analysis and Application

If The Player is T.W.T.B.H, he uses the Base Runner method to filter out problems and progress forward in a measurable way. The Player learns how to master The Game by controlling his actions, being mindful of his motives and capturing the power that comes with self-control. The Player using the Base Runner method avoids traps, pitfalls, and setbacks. He avoids unnecessary commitment, deception, and arguments where behavior has to be explained.

The Base Runner method is based off the concept of First Base, Second Base, Third Base and Home Plate. Each base represents a phase The Player must go through to reach sexual gratification. First base is the kiss. Second base is making out. Third base is the phase where genitals are touched. Home base is sexual penetration. If these phases sound old-school and contrary to the trends of today, that is because they are. Sexual penetration without going through the proper screening process can lead to major losses in The Game. Having sex with a woman only to find out there are no commonalities for growth can be avoided by using the Base Runner method. This method allows The Player to investigate a potential teammate to ensure that she is the one he is ready to give his God's

"The study of everyday life reveals to us how humans can act creatively to shape reality. Although social behavior is guided to some extent by forces such as rules, norms and shared expectations, individuals perceive reality differently according to their backgrounds interests and motivations."

Introducing Communication Theory Analysis and Application

Power, or GP.

The goal of The Game is for The Player to build his legacy and the Base Runner method allows him to find his sidekick. This method allows The Player to get to know a young lady without making physical commitments. Physical commitments tend to lead to distracting obligations and possibly a dissonance between The Player and the lady. Applying this method also ensures that The Player meets the lady's standard.

It takes a great deal of energy for The Player to give a lady his GP. This energy is not limited to the physical energy exerted by The Player during orgasm. The energy he must put forth to get to Home Base must also be considered. Putting into play the Base Runner method, The Player is able to get a glimpse of whether a lady will be supportive not just in words but in actions as well. It is best for The Player to know that the lady is down for the goal and his methodology before he gives her his body.

Take for instance the rapper who has sex with the woman that does not know any of his songs. If he is giving his body to a woman who does not listen to his music, he will fall short in his success. In this case, The Player is actually

Anderson asked Goffman what type of behavior cues and signs make up public interaction? He concluded that; Skin color, gender, companions, clothing, jewelry, and objects that people carry help indentify so that assumptions are formed and communication can occur. Movements (quick or slow, sincere, comprehensible or incomprehensible) further refine public communication."

working against himself. He is giving his GP to someone who does not believe in him. The Player should never doubt himself and should surround himself with people who also believe in him. If The Player is having sex with a woman who doubts his gift, this will lead to The Player hearing negative and doubtful words. This results in unnecessary problems and adversity.

"Basic modes of emotional expression are the same in all human beings."

Introducing Communication Theory Analysis and Application

The Base Runner Method

First Base	The Player is interested in finding out more and rewards a lady with a kiss.
Second Base	"The Making Out Phase" represents the realization of physical attraction. In this stage, The Player showcases passion by the intensity of kiss and the intimacy of his touch. A hug becomes more than a hug and a kiss is more than a kiss but it is still controlled and measured.
Third Base	"Show and Tell" is the phase in which the genitals are explored through the touching of hands. The Player and lady learn how each other like to be intimately touched, mind and body connect through communication and action.
Home Base	This represents sexual penetration. Protected or unprotected, anally or vaginally are all covered in this phase. If he and a lady reach this level, it should be because The Player wants her to be his main partner.

Power of a Question

"For lack of guidance a nation falls, but many advisers make victory sure."

"When Pride comes, then comes a disgrace, but with humility comes wisdom."

There is a power that lies within The Player that will light his way. Through this power, the doors of opportunity will present themselves and the accumulation of Jewels will become a daily success. It is the Power of a Question, or POQ.

POQ is the ability of The Player to tap into the power of using "What", "When", "Where", "Why", and "How" to discover truth. Discovering knowledge, wisdom, and understanding through POQ is empowering and will lead to transcending to higher of levels of The Game. POQ is a powerful tool in The Player's toolkit. It is as if The Player is a gold digger and each person he meets is a new plot of land. His "Hows" and "Whats" are his shovel and pick, digging and investigating each person for potential gold. Once The Player uses POQ and discovers the first bits of treasure, he digs deeper and builds upon his discovery. Upon this discovery, The Player begins to build a relationship in which he can accumulate more Jewels.

"Our lives are organized around the repetition of similar patterns of behavior."

Introducing Communication Theory Analysis and Application

POQ allows The Player to accumulate Jewels daily while building bridges. It all starts when he introduces himself and initiates a conversation by asking the other person how he or she is doing. The Player is always concerned for others because he wants others to be concerned for him. A King cares for his people and in return the people care for and love the King. By asking a person how he or she is doing, The Player begins the art of using his five senses as a way to investigate the person with his Eye of Observation and Investigation. The Player continues to use POQ to dig even deeper with follow up questions. He may say "I see you are dressed up; where are you headed?" Or, "I see you just got off work; how are things at the job?" The more he asks, the more he learns.

"When a mocker is punished, the simple gain wisdom; by paying attention to the wise they get knowledge."

Ecclesiastes 19:11 NIV

As The Player continues to investigate in this manner, he is showing concern for others. When he does this, an amazing new thing happens. The people The Player showed concern for will begin to show concern for him. The Player will find that more often than not, asking a person how they are doing will result in that person answering and reflecting the question back to The Player. The love The Player showed to another is directly reflected back to him.

This understanding of reflection is the basic foundation of

POQ that The Player has to build upon. He needs to understand that when he uses POQ, it will be reflected back at him. At the same time The Player is accumulating Jewels, he also has the ability to display his own Jewels.

The Player can use this understanding of reflection to his advantage. When he wants to show and prove his knowledge and understanding, instead of pressing to tell people, he just asks the right questions that will lead the person reflecting the question back to him. This is the best time for The Player to say what he has to say because he was asked directly for his opinion. The Player now knows for a fact that the person wants to hear what The Player has to say because he asked. This is the perfect time for The Player to showcase his own Jewels.

"After all, the only thing a man knows is himself. The world outside he can know only by hear-say."

Alexander Smith

Even if The Player does not know the answer to a question he is asked, he can show humbleness in stating he does not know and would like to learn. In fact, the very nature of POQ requires The Player to put his pride aside and take on the role of student. Life is a learning experience and using POQ gives him the ability to enhance the experience on a daily basis.

The Player can also use the concept of reflection when he

has a problem. As he goes about his daily routine of asking people how they are doing, The Player should express his problem in the form of a question when his question is reflected back at him. If The Player is having trouble tying his shoe, when he is asked how he is doing he responds by saying, "I'm frustrated. I am trying to figure out HOW to tie my shoe. Do you mind helping me?" This is completely different from answering with, "I'm mad because I can't tie this shoe. Can you do it for me?"

In the first situation, The Player shows humility. He expresses how frustrated he is, that he does not know how to tie his shoe but would like to learn. He never says that he cannot do it, but rather that he does not know how. Secondly, The Player has a desire to learn how to tie his shoe, not simply have someone else do it for him. The question is intentionally worded this way in order to be provided with a solution.

"He who guards his lips guards his life, but he who speaks rashly will come to ruin."

Proverbs 13:3 NIV

In the second situation, The Player paints himself as helpless and in need of someone to tie his shoes for him. There is no sense of wanting to do it himself or to learn how it is done. This way of thinking is extremely unappealing. The Player should always want to know how something is done, even if he cannot do it himself. There may come a time in the future when the knowledge may be needed.

The Player also uses POQ to exhibit self-control in the face of an argument. This is very important, especially when engaging women. Words are the weapons of women; The Player must use POQ to gain clarity. He uses POQ and his Eye of Observation and Investigation to find the truth behind what women are saying instead of assuming or arguing. The Player states what he knows and then investigates what the woman knows about the situation.

"Do not be quickly provoked in your spirit, for anger resides in the lap of fools."

Ecclesiastes 7:9 NIV

This is another example of why The Player needs to be confident in his own self-knowledge in the face of a woman. The Player needs to know what he is talking about. He should know himself and his understanding so as not to be lead astray. Women have an ability to say things that make men operate in their emotions rather than logic. They know how to strike a chord in a man that will make him go against what he knows to be right. The Player must be aware of this power and investigate what a woman is saying and her intentions thoroughly. Eve does not have the ability to see the whole picture. She only sees a portion of something, and that portion is usually what will directly affect her in the present. She may say that she is thinking for the betterment of everyone, but upon further investigation, The Player may notice that her motivations are completely selfish. Women are naturally emotional, and so they use the power of words to get men to operate in a state of being that is comfortable and controlling for the woman. The Player uses POQ to keep himself grounded and aware so he can make the right decision.

By using POQ, The Player displays his ability to learn and his inclination to know better. It then falls upon The Player to make the right choices regarding governance and level selection. Ignorance of how he should carry himself is no excuse. With POQ, The Player can always learn how to govern himself in any given situation and can also show that he knows why he is doing something when the question is reflected back to him. From there, it becomes the responsibility of The Player to choose the high road. After using POQ to investigate the situation, he uses his knowledge of self and T.W.T.B.H. to take on the challenge of the high road.

There will always be a low road and a high road that The Player can take in any situation. Both are difficult, one just appears easy and provides instant gratification while the other involves self-control, patience and work. The easy

"Do not be over righteous, neither be over wise— Why destroy yourself? Do not be over wicked, and do not be a fool—why die before your time? It is good to grasp the one and not let go of the other. Whoever fears God will avoid all extremes. Wisdom makes one wise person more powerful than ten rulers in a city."

Ecclesiastes 7:16 – 19 NIV

path always ends up costing more in the end and the path that appears harder always pays off in the end. There is no getting around it.

When using POQ, The Player is naturally using his eyes and ears. He uses his mind and his journal to analyze the information. Taking in information, writing it down, analyzing it for Jewels, and then making decisions are all major parts of game play. POQ makes the process easier and can be applied in a targeted manner in which The Player gains access directly to the desired level. The Game is all about acquiring Jewels to gain entrance to the higher levels. If The Player just asks, he shall receive. It again comes back to The Player knowing himself and knowing his wants and needs. At a certain point, it does not matter if The Player does not want something if he continues to ask for it. If he asks for it, whether he wants it or not, he will receive it. There is truth in the saying "be careful what you wish for, you might just get it." It is the same thing with The Game. The Player needs to be mindful of what he asks for; he just might get it.

"Self-knowledge comes from knowing other men."

Johann Wolfgang von-Goethe

While accumulating Jewels with the POQ, The Player will also have the opportunity to acquire Eve. If he knows what he wants, and uses the POQ, he can find the Eve that exhibits the qualities that he is looking for. It all comes back to knowledge of self. If The Player loves to eat, and he has a choice between two women, he should find out which one can cook. He asks the hard questions. If The Player is destined for this journey to become a King, is she down to help carry the weight of the world on their shoulders? Does she know what forever means, and is she down for eternity?

"Self-reverence, self-knowledge, self-control - These three alone lead to power."

Alfred Lord Tennyson

The Player uses the POQ to discover the intentions of women and their inner motives. He asks basic questions to find out her sign and favorite book, color, television show, childhood memory. What type of dreams and aspirations does she have? What are her vices and virtues? The Player uses POQ to evaluate how Eve sees herself. This also gives him a chance to learn the woman. Maya Angelo said it best when she stated, "When someone shows you who they are believe them; the first time."

POQ gives Eve the opportunity to show herself. The Player needs to know if Eve has the qualities needed to reflect his inner qualities, so he asks. Conversations about childhood to parenthood are opportunities for The Player to use POQ to learn about Eve and the capacity to see past her exterior. Because of Eve's nature of reflection, she will ask the questions back to The Player. This is his opportunity to showcase his acquired Jewels. By taking the time to learn the inside of Eve, she will take the time to admire his Jewels, the substance of which he wants her to make her decision. So begins the process of choosing.

How the team interacts with The Player is also based on how he uses POQ. If The Player respects his teammates and uses POQ to learn from them, the team will work better. If The Player always seems to know it all and does not listen to the input of his team, he will come to ruin. He may seem to be an independent success but life is a team game. If the overall team is not winning, then The Player's glory will be limited. Independent accolades are nice for the Lad Phase but for the Adam and King Phases, it is all about team work. Winning as a team has substance and establishes the footpath of a legacy.

"The success of teamwork coming together is a beginning; keeping together is progress working together is success."

Henry Ford

The thirst to be a better, more effective and efficient player in The Game is quenched by using POQ. The Player chooses to open himself to new levels of The Game and greater understanding simply by asking questions. There is a well-known phrase that puts it simply: a closed mouth don't get fed. If The Player does not ask, he leaves himself no other choice but to assume and when The Player assumes, he makes an "ass" of "u" and "me." The Player works to be the man who asks the hard questions, the ones that prepare him for the harsh realities of life, so he knows how to govern himself.

As The Player plays The Game and meets people through his daily interactions, he should use POQ as a way to discover his role in the different arenas in his life. He should use it to be the best player he can be in all aspects of life including school, work, hobbies, and The Game. The Player should use it to discover what is required of him and the best way to live up to these expectations. He can then use the knowledge and wisdom accumulated to make the right decisions, which lead to success and furtherance in The Game. The Player must realize that by asking questions, he can avoid the pitfalls of those who came before him regardless of the arena.

"You get in life what you have the courage to ask for."

Oprah Winfrey

Chapter Review

- The Power of a Question (POQ) is tapping into the power of "what, when, where, why, and how" to discover truth and to accumulate Jewels for The Game.
- The Player uses POQ to learn his environment and the rules of governance. He asks questions to discover who is on his team, who is his coach, and his opponent.
- POQ can open the door to direct accumulation of Jewels and advancement in levels. By asking, The Player opens the door to receive.
- The Player uses POQ in combination with his Eye of Observation and Investigation and his journal to analyze the Jewels accumulated.
- Through the process of using POQ, The Player displays humility as well as being given a chance to display his acquired Jewels.
- The Player can find and learn the nature of his Eve through the use of POQ. The Player can learn how and why his woman perceives reality the way she does.
- The Player can use POQ to control himself in an argument, by using the opportunity to listen and learn instead of talk and fight.
- The Player can use the POQ to be a better team player by learning from his teammates.

Strategies

Now that The Player is familiar with The Game and his purpose, he needs tips on how to maneuver through it. This section opens the door to jewels of insight on how to play The Game with the Big Head. These strategies are to be used be as instruments for clarity into the previous sections of the book. These Jewels are to be broken down into three sections: Fine Silver, Choice Gold, and Precious Rubies.

The Jewels in this section of the book will illuminate the different levels of The Game and the different situations The Player may face. The insight will come in forms of self-correction, understandings of women and The Game. The Player will be able to see how The Game unfolds and the importance of Thinking with the Big Head.

Fine Silver

Fix Yourself

We all go through life wanting to fix things about ourselves. Sometimes we are in situations in life in which we recognize lifestyle traits and situations that don't make us happy and we want to change them. The problem is figuring out how to change and the motivation to change. There are 5 easy steps that will welcome change and help bring a pool of motivation to get it done. With that being said, there are new things that you need to add into your daily regimen.

Step 1. Get a journal. Write about you. Write about your needs, wants, goals, aspirations, loves, and hates. This is the place you can say what you want and how you want without judgment. Most importantly, this is where you can clearly define who you are and what your goals are. This is where you can articulate the problems you have with yourself and how to deal with them.

Step 2. Read a book. It is important that some reading and conscious learning take place. Notes can be taken in the journal. It is important that you take the time to investigate a solution outside of what you already know. If for some reason you have a problem with reading, watch a credible source on YouTube.

Step 3. Distance yourself from those you recognize are not benefiting you. You need givers, not takers. You need guidance and wisdom. You need people who have been where you are going, or who have been where you have been, and have the understanding to look back and share wisdom. If the people you are around now were going to help you get to where you wanted to go, you'd be there already.

Step 4. Make an effort to surround yourself with people that support your dreams and represent your goals and aspirations. The people that you associate yourself with should represent the character traits that you admire and accept. Birds of a feather should flock together. Recognize the roles and purpose that the people in your life serve and decide whether or not they are fulfilling them.

Step 5. Research your Creator. Research who you believe created you. Why? If you know what created you, then you could understand why you were created, and possibly reach out to the Creator to change his creation. This is very important. If you have a relationship with your Creator, then you could reach out to it for help to do the "impossible." It is the Creator, of course the "impossible" can be done.

It is up to you recognize and follow the signs to get to the end, but using these methods the path will be clearer.

*Using Thinking with the Big Head will directly help you see and follow the signs in life to achieve your life goals

If You Don't Like It, Don't Choose It

If you hate it, then you hate it. If you don't like something, then you don't like it. If you tell somebody that you don't like something but then choose it and come back complaining, what do you think they are going to say to you?

The question that is posed in this lesson is:
If you don't like something, then why would you choose it?

If a woman does not offer you any substance, why would you sleep with her continuously? If you are always talking about something that you do not like about this person, why would you continue to sleep with her? Also, think about what it is that you may have to go through just to get the physical pleasure.

If you recognize that you don't like someone and you continue to sleep with her, eventually something disastrous will take place. If someone is always pulling you down and seems only to bring you physical pleasure, then you are headed directly for the bottom. If you give your body and energy to something that has the weight to pull you down and not the energy to push you up, you will eventually fall. This is why it is important to keep your scissors sharp. I doubt that you will fall in love with someone that you do not like.

To bring this home just imagine this thought. You are on the third floor of a 10 story building and you get on the elevator. You press the number 1 but you want to go to 10. Everything you want to do is on 10th floor, but you pressed the button for the 1st floor. On which floor will the doors open? You got it.

KNOW BETTER, DO BETTER, AND CHOOSE BETTER.

Power UP.

Get What You Ask For

Asking questions is a very important tool in The Game. Asking questions brings clarity and awareness to a situation or need. Asking questions acts as a filter to screen out undesirables, fakes, and tricksters/deceivers. Also, asking questions has the ability to reveal the intentions of others in The Game.

First and foremost, Thinking with the Big Head means never assuming; it is always better to ask. To assume is to act as if one possesses all knowledge and wisdom of a situation. It is better to ask a person about a situation than to assume to know their answer. It is better to ask for clarity or whether assistance is needed than to assume to fully understand or to be unprepared.

"A closed mouth don't get fed," is a lesson my mother used to preach. In the process of asking, The Player opens himself up for reception. He admits that he has a lacking and puts himself in the mental mind-state to receive. The process of asking for help is, in itself, reaching out to the universe and searching for the answer. By asking other people for what it is he seeks, The Player finds directions, assistance, and ultimately the thing in which he seeks. By opening his mouth, he begins the process of filling a lack that he has.

When asking, The Player must be mindful of what it he is asking for. The saying "be mindful what you ask for, you might just get it," is very important. This means it is important to be mindful of what is asked for because it might not be what it appears. A lot of people ask for fame and when they receive it they cannot deal with what comes with it. Fame looks good, but is it as good as it looks? The Player must recognize when he has found what it is he seeks, and not a fake or a trap. How does The Player do this? How does The Player deploy his Eye of Investigation and Observation? By asking questions. The Player uses the P.O.Q. to find truth and understanding. He uses the P.O.Q. to figure out the situation and the best way to govern himself in a way to win. The P.O.Q. is his go to move to make sure everything goes smoothly and that he understands the game fully. He asks questions such as "Is everything ok?", "Did I do this right?", and most importantly, "What do you think?" These questions help bring insight to what others think, and these thoughts are the keys to the truth. The only way The Player can truly gain access is by asking.

Take this situation for example. One day I was at a hotel and I met a Lady of the Night. Upon investigation, the Lady revealed to me that she was also a thief. If she thought she was not treated right, she would not hesitate to help herself to what was not given to her and this was quite often. Was she physically appealing? Was she a possible money making situation? Would she have liked the presence and company of the Governor? Yes, to all three. Was she worth it? No, plain and simple. This young lady was investigated and she was deemed a physically appealing bunch of problems, problems that would have cost more than any amount of money she could have made. Any type of sexual encounter would have surely bred a demon that would have haunted me. I inquired by asking, and the truth was revealed. I did not assume. My principles teach me that nothing good comes from stealing, and by her own admission, she acknowledges that nothing good will come from her. So why bother?

Another example, but on the opposite end of the spectrum, is a man that asked me a question. I was buying books when I asked the gentleman if he could help me move a box of books I was purchasing. He said yes, and after he was finished, he asked me is there anything else he could help me with. I asked him if he wanted a job and he said yes. At that moment, Agent Drew was born. Again, we can see the advantage of asking questions. This situation was entirely different but the process yielded the same results. It does not matter how much a person may want something, he will always get it faster by asking than by waiting for someone to just give it to him. I needed help, and when someone offered to fulfill that need, I stepped up and asked them to do it. By that I mean, I needed a worker, and when someone asked me if I needed help, I asked them directly for what I needed. I did not allow the context of being in the library buying books limit how this person could help me.

By asking, I received exactly what I was looking for. I exercised the Power of a Question and found what I was looking for. I went to the Lady of the Night for material, and that's exactly what I found - material for a blog. Find and get what you seek by using the Power of a Question.

Find the One

I recently received an email that said, "Gov, how do I find the one?"

The answer is Know Thy Self. In the process of knowing thyself, you will find the one. She should be the one that makes you strive for greatness in whatever is your purpose and gives the most motivation in action, not just words. Take action over words every time.

How does this come about functionally? By answering the following questions: What do you know about yourself? What makes you special? What do you like to do and what is your future? What is your favorite color, song, astrological sign? What are your philosophical beliefs? What do you like to eat? Where and how do you want to live?

In the process of answering these questions and in the actions it takes to live by them in the physical world, is where you will find your woman. She will be there, and by using the P.O.Q. and knowing the answers you seek, you will find that special one.

You need to know what you can and cannot tolerate. By answering some of the aforementioned questions, you will discover truths that can guide you in the right direction. You need to know your nature so you can know what it is that you tend to do because you are the man and the leader. You need to know you have a partner who knows your ways and can recognize when you stray and help you get back on track. Your special person only wants the best for you and should step in if she sees you doing something that is out of character.

To sum it up, the answer to the question "how do I find that special one?" is Know Thyself. In this journey the one will make herself known, and it is up to you overcome the challenges in making her yours. Use P.O.Q. and "Stand Strong," and the one will be yours.

Watch Your Words

Law 16 in the 48 Laws of Power by Robert Greene instructs us to "Use absence to increase presence." This lesson is about using actions instead of words to express how you feel when you are upset. Women love words. So give them words to express love, loyalty and commitment. You use words to express the dream. You use actions to enforce them. In casual conversation you may state what you do when you get upset, but when you get upset, you are all about action.

Words are a double edged sword. They can be used verbally, or in writing (i.e. love notes, poems, etc.), which will help drive your message directly to a lady's heart. On the other side of the sword are the words that can be said when upset. Those words have the opportunity to burn directly to the soul. I must give an important message here in all caps. IF A WOMAN SAYS HURTFUL THINGS ABOUT YOUR FAMILY MEMBERS, YOU SHOULD LEAVE HER ALONE. IF SHE CALLS YOU NAMES AND YOUR FAMILY MEMBERS NAMES, YOU SHOULD LEAVE HER IMMEDIATELY. Those women will cause you to go to jail. If a woman calls your mother a bitch, you should leave her right then at that second. If you want to be funny, you can throw a drink in her face. Actions not words. No hitting or physical contact. Drink throwing and walking away.

You can't win with words when you are upset. Don't try. If you are on the phone, hang up and cut the phone off as soon you sense things are getting out of hand. If you have to continue to repeat what you are saying or finding yourself trying to justify yourself, don't say anything. Walk away. Go sleep on the couch. If she is the type who likes to follow you and yell, just walk straight out the door, and just keep walking. Walking should be your best friend. Mental toughness in this area will be exponentially beneficial.

Don't be fearful. There is an old saying that should sustain you while you are on your walk: “Time heals all wounds.” If I cut the phone off, it won’t be the worst that could happen. If I get home and she acts crazy, I’ll just go for a walk. Time can do more than your words can. If you messed up, don't say anything. Always avoid arguing by walking away and denying a person communication for an extended amount of time. For example, volunteer to sleep on the couch for a week or so. Only communicate the essentials, making sure to say good morning, how are you doing but that's about it. Nothing else. You are mad and you show it by not talking at all. You don't get mad and scream. You get mad and walk away.

To ensure you get your point across, you have to understand why you are upset so that every time your woman asks what is wrong, you can say one or two things to her that you want changed and stick to them. You will get the change that made you upset.

Put What You Do Well First

In order to do well in this world, you must put what you do well first.

- What is it that you do well?
- Are you able to lose yourself in this action?
- How often do you share this gift with the world?

The lesson of the week teaches us that in order to do well in this world we must put first what we do well. Through the learning and practice of our gift, we can bring peace and substance to life. We can find ourselves and our purpose through the practice of our gift. Learning how to use our gift for the betterment of the world is a journey unto itself that can give an individual purpose.

The process starts with the individual taking a hard look in the mirror, applying the Eye of Observation and Investigation and asking "What am I good at? What is it that I do that brings me a sense of accomplishment?" There should be a thorough investigation into one's self to find the gift.

The next step in the process is researching the gift. This should be an ongoing, lifelong process. Researching and learning about the gift from within should be an ongoing practice that a person does as they grow in life. The research and learning will prepare you to use your gift and to help you evolve your gift to its highest level. In research and learning, you can begin to find your own way to use your gift. Research and learning entails finding out as much as you can about the physical and spiritual nature of the gift. Learn about those in the past who have been able to master gifts similar to your own. Learning from others gives us a reference point for methods and perceptions of the gift. Learn the pitfalls they faced, and how the world received them. All of this knowledge and wisdom will provide for the proper preparation for the world.

The most important part of research and learning is learning the opposite side of the gift. There is an ancient saying; "the gift and the curse,'' and it shows us that there is a correlation of the gift with a curse. The curse is the downside or burden that comes with the gift. The research and learning phase is the best time to learn about the curse of the gift. The majority of the time, the greater the gift, the greater the burden. It is best to learn the gift and the curse in the research and learning stage instead of being blind-sided and having to learn through raw experience. It is always better to be prepared for the obstacles in life than to face them clueless.

In the process of research and learning, one will find oneself. The process of research and learning is the process of gaining knowledge of self. Knowledge of self is empowering. The empowering knowledge can be fuel for greatness. By taking time to research and learn the gift, its practices and its power, a plan can be formed to bring the gift to the world. A journal is most definitely needed in this stage. As knowledge is gained and awareness is achieved, all should be written down. The gift and all thoughts surrounding it should be written down. It will be the initial wall that ideas and ways of the gift are bounced off of.

Take a builder for example. He is born with an inner urge to build. He would grow into his craft and learn about King Solomon, the Master Builder. He would read and study knowledge of the craft. He would look to other buildings for inspiration, take notes and then he would build. From the practice of building comes the urge to share the buildings with the world. There begins the process of sharing the gift with the world.

As one begins to engage in the gift, an urge will grow within you, an urge to showcase this gift to the world. This problem is easily solved through Eye C U. The hard part is making the choice to give the gift to the world, understanding that it will be rewarding but difficult. Finding time and energy to give the gift can be difficult at times. The gift in itself may be time consuming and difficult but the teaching is that "in order to do well in this world, we must put what you do well first." Either you deal with the challenge of giving the world the gift and having purpose, or you deal with the dissonance of keeping the gift to yourself. With the latter choice comes a sense of depression, hopelessness and lack of purpose. Overcoming the physical and lower-self and sharing the light of the gift is fulfilling. To share the gift and to receive love for it is the most ultimate feeling that one can experience.

To recap:

- "To do well in this world, we put must what we do well first."

- Look in the mirror and use the Eye of Observation and Investigation to find the gift or gifts.

- Research and learn the gift and curse. Learn knowledge, wisdom and understanding on the gift. Learn of others with the gift.

- Practice and engage in the gift and do not ignore the urge to share it with the world.

Choice Gold

A Woman's Curse

Curse

noun \ˈkərs\

- an offensive word that people say when they are angry
- magical words that are said to cause trouble or bad luck for someone or the condition that results when such words are said
- a cause of trouble or bad luck

"Heaven has no rage like love to hatred turned, Nor hell a fury like a woman scorned" – The Mourning Bride, *William Congreve*

Have you been having bad luck lately or noticed a string of bad events happening in your life that seem outside of your control but seem to be directly affecting your plans? If you want to know the source of these happenings, look no further than the women in your life. Think about what you may have said or done that may have caused one of the women in your life to put a curse on you. Maybe that ex-girlfriend that you hit up when you were horny? Or your baby momma who always has attitude? Or your friend with benefits who harbors a certain feeling? This is a very important lesson if you are into underground activities, are a major businessman or a dream chaser. If you do not pay attention, a curse could be put on you that will lead to death, incarceration, or poverty.

T.W.T.B.H. teaches that we are the makers of our reality. When we use our Little Head to make decisions there is often a price we pay later down the road for those decisions. When we operate with our Little Head when dealing with ladies, we tend to evoke lower-self emotions in these ladies. So when the ladies get upset with you, do they curse you? Do they tell you something negative will happen? Do they swear that they will get you back or that you will feel exactly how they feel or worse? Do they call you names and use words that evoke negative spirits in you? Just think about what happens in your mind and body after you have a passionate argument with a woman in your life. What do you do afterwards? Have you ever done anything destructive to yourself after having an argument with your woman, or has anything negative happened shortly after an argument with a woman?

The purpose of this lesson and knowledge is to help you govern yourself in the future. It is knowledge and wisdom to prevent you from engaging in passionate arguments and saying something that you will regret. It will also help you recognize what it is a woman is saying when she gets upset. You should stop her in her tracks when she says something damning. If she wishes some sort of bad luck or misfortune on you, you make her take it back or apologize for saying it. Better yet, do not engage her to the point where she is so upset enough to say and do things that will have long lasting effects. It is up to you to realize what is going on when the situation is going down.

According to Edward Cayce, every thought builds our reality. If this is the case, then we create our reality simply by believing it. With this in mind, we should be careful what we believe. Thoughts and words have power. If you know anything about women, you know that whenever something bad happens they love to talk about it. They love to sit and think about it and dwell in the past. So, in essence, when a woman gets upset at you and you push her to the point where she starts to swear and curse you, you need to be aware that negativity in life can become your reality if you don't handle the situation properly. When a woman curses you, she is serious and she wants you to feel the pain that she is placing upon you. Does she know that how she makes you feel she will end up reliving herself? No, she doesn't understand that by cursing you she is cursing herself, but that's irrelevant. When you push a woman to that point, she is hurt and that is when they are the most powerful. If she uses this power to make you feel bad, you will feel bad. Women are at work while you sleep. They are at work while you are at work. They are at work while you are sitting on the shitter. When you see bad happening in your life there is probably a woman somewhere celebrating.

Also, because of a woman's nature to talk to other women about her problems, there may be a force of two or more against you. Women tend to give women advice that is not always in the man's favor. And since you have pushed this woman to this level she is going to go seek out help. This help may come in the form of a girlfriend, a lawyer, the police, an ex or future boyfriend. All these people are looking to bring negativity to your life. All these people are tools for this woman to use to bring pain into your life.

The key points to take from this lesson are:

- The women in your life can curse you and manifest real world consequences.
- The words that come from these women when they are hurt can affect you even when they are not expressed directly to you. How women talk about

you when you are not around is more important than when you are around. When you hurt a woman and she curses you to anyone who listens and wishes ill fortune upon you, it can manifest itself in your life.

- Words and thoughts are powerful. Thoughts and words have a real tangible effect that can be felt in the physical world. With that in mind, we need to be mindful of the energy that comes our way. We need to be mindful of the women in our lives and how they feel towards us.

This next part is very important!

If you are giving yourself sexually to a woman who is cursing you, you will increase the power of her curses to manifest in your life. You are giving her a doorway to enter your inner sanctum of thought and an opportunity to plant a bomb that she can blow up at will.

I hope this understanding will shine light upon why something in your life happened that you could not understand. When I tell you that vagina is not free, I mean it is not free. Power UP.

A Woman's Sad Story

A woman with a sad story can be dangerous. In my travels and upon investigation, I have learned that a woman uses a sad story to run game on men. She has the ability to use a man's generosity and sexual attraction to her against him. A woman with a constant sad story will use a man up and move on to another man with more resources. Or she will disappear until the man has fresh resources for her to ask for.

Has a woman ever come to you in need of immediate assistance or help? Have you ever dealt with a woman who was sexually appealing but always found themselves in a situation where they needed help or assistance? Did they always feel the world was not fair or extremely harsh towards them?

As understood in Thinking with the Big Head, a woman's weapon is her words. A woman with a sad story uses her words as a weapon to make a man give up his resources. A man that a woman recognizes will give out without anything in return other than sex is known as a "trick." The woman acts as if she cares for the man, then hits him with a sad story followed by a request for resources. The favor can be anything from a ride to money, to even purchasing of materials. The man thinks he is helping and being good, while she is thinking he is a fool.

If a man uses his P.O.Q.(Power of a Question), he can begin to see through the deception. He can also learn how to give help without being considered a "trick." Assistance comes with strings attached and those strings cannot be sex. Sex is the temptation that makes the words the woman use have weight. She uses the sexual attraction and the will to see her happy against the man to the point where she no longer considers his situation or what something may cost him. She only cares about her sad story. If a man falls for this he will become a pawn.

If a woman sincerely wants help from a gentleman, she will listen and let him lead her to a better way. If she asks for assistance to be used in a way that she sees fit, or wants to do it her way, he is being set up. He is being used as a "trick." A woman does not respect a "trick." A woman does not love a "trick" and will leave him in the wind, assed out. The only time she protects the trick is if she recognizes her plan is in danger.

Recognize the sad story for what it is; it is an opportunity for man to use his resources to get somewhere with a woman. Using the Power of a Question, a man can check out the situation and see if hc is able to help under *his* conditions. If not, he says no. He knows that a woman can use a sad story to take advantage of a man, and so he recognizes that the plea is not genuine. If a woman wants help from a man, she will allow him to do it his way and will not create the sense of urgency that she should handle the situation. He should never blindly trust a sad story that he cannot help directly. Any favors that are paid with sex, or done with the intentions of sex, puts a man in the "trick" zone, a zone that will gain him no respect or love.

Choose the Best for You

"Why did you choose me? Why did I choose you? Thinking with the Big Head teaches that I should have chosen you because you are the best because you bring out the best in me." Governor

In America, we have the free will to choose our mates. **T.W.T.B.H. teaches that a man learns his purpose and looks for a mate to help achieve this goal. T.W.T.B.H. teaches that a man gives his body to the woman who makes his dreams come true, the woman who decides to dedicate herself to achieving this man's goals as her own.** T.W.T.B.H. teaches a man that he does not settle for something that merely looks good but actually chooses the best by its substance.

Every man is born to be great. He is born to be great to his team/family. By being the best for the family, he is preparing to be the best for the world. Any mate the man chooses should help him be the best man he can be for his family. A mate has to be down for the family. There is no getting around this. When you are giving your time and energy to something, it must benefit the whole. **You should be mindful of giving yourself to something that leads you away from your team (family) or your goal.**

When you understand that you are meant to be great, you understand that your woman has to see and acknowledge your greatness. What does the world look like thinking you are great but the person who shares your bed believes you are a peasant? Your woman must recognize your Kingship, because you are a King.

The Governor is telling you that you are a King in your world. You must recognize that even a King humbles himself to his creators, which would be God and your father, the words of the man who will always ring in your ears. This is your world and your father created you. That's why it is important to understand where you came from so you can know where you are going. This journey is something that you do not take alone. This is a mission that you take with a woman of your choosing, and through this journey you build the bonds of love.

This mission is an example of a path that can be taken with a woman in order for her to prove herself. If you play a sport, this woman should help you become the best and greatest. She should understand that it is your mission to achieve and she needs to be the boost when the world is weighing heavy. She should be the one who looks you in the eye and in that moment you feel your greatness, you know that you can do it.

The woman that you choose to give yourself to will become a mirror of you. She can either reflect your deficiencies or your greatness. T.W.T.B.H. teaches that she should reflect your greatness. She should reflect your awesome ability. Why? Because you chose her. You chose her because you understood that with her natural qualities and your nature, together you can take it to the next level. You deserve the best and you chose the best. She had the special abilities to do the things you could not and you do the things that she cannot. Together you make an unstoppable tandem that will achieve the heights of greatness.

Hard Head Makes A Soft A**

My mother always told me "a hard head makes a soft ass." I'd like to build on these wise words with you. Thinking with the Big Head teaches us that we should take the wise words that people give us and apply them. So the Governor is here to tell you that when your mother tells you "leave that girl alone, she is trouble," you need to listen. Your mother is not going to tell you anything wrong. And yes, she will always want to be the number one woman in your life and she should. But if your mother tells you she is trouble, leave that woman alone.

Your mother loves you and has the ability to prophecy in your life. Your mother will not deny you a woman that she knows that is good for you. There is a difference between a woman that your mother doesn't like, and a woman that your mother says is "bad for you." Personality differences can be worked on, but if your mother knows a woman has negative intentions for her son, she is going to fight it, and she is supposed to.

No matter what happens in a man's life while growing up, he normally looks to his mother for comfort and support. Do not sacrifice the love and understanding of your mother for a woman. If she loves you, she has to love or have some love towards your mother, considering she created you. THIS IS VERY IMPORTANT...IF YOUR MOTHER SAYS "LEAVE THAT WOMAN ALONE, SHE IS TROUBLE".....LEAVE HER ALONE. You do not know more than your mother. You do not know her better than she does. You don't know her better than I do, and I am telling you to leave her alone. "A hard head makes a soft ass."

Choices and the Game

The Game of Life comes down to one word and that word is......choices. Choice or choices are the deciding factors of The Game. What The Player does when the ball is in his hands or the move he makes to spring the big play are just examples of the importance of The Player's choices. The player makes Game altering decisions in the blink of an eye and must be mindful of them and their reactions. Just imagine The Player in the game who scores by instinct. He feels a slight discomfort every time he misses a shot and it can take a toll on his morale.

The choices we make in life are as simple as good and bad. Good choices have long term benefits and bad choices don't. The immediate pleasure of a decision is not the deciding factor of whether the choice was a good one or bad one. Just because something feels good, doesn't mean it is a good choice. It could feel good one minute, and then cause a lifetime of pain. That would be viewed as an overall bad decision or choice.

When The Player makes the right choices, the game falls into play. But when he makes bad decisions, The Game is forced. When The Player plays the game right, long term good opportunities will present themselves. But with bad decisions comes instant gratification but long term discomfort, unnecessary difficulties, and ultimately they will lead to losses.

The Player will have to decide what are wins and losses and this will directly depend on the goal. Certain things just come with the accomplishment of goals.

The temptations of fame, power, and sex are commonalities of success and victory. Certain happenings in The Game are just costs of the goal, just as prison is the cost of an illegal game. If a man makes a bunch of money selling drugs, balls out and lives the high life, but then gets a lengthy prison sentence, he then pays the true cost of the high life.

Choices are like credit cards; you use them now, gain an experience and then pay later. The major difference between the two is the speed of usage. The Player makes so many decisions that he loses track of when it is time to pay for them. The Player goes through experiences that are payments for decisions previously made, and sometimes he forgets those initial decisions. This causes The Player dissonance because he may be experiencing hard or tough times and can't figure out why. He should look to his past decisions and efforts. He should look at past methods and intentions and what were the consequences. He should find the answers there.

Choices are what The Game is all about. To be a winner in the game, The Player must make the most out of his opportunity by making good decisions. To achieve this goal, The Player must learn, study, and most importantly...practice. If The Player practices making good decisions, he will develop a habit of doing so. As long as he remains humble and reads the signs, he can win with grace and leave the game in honor....Power UP

Precious Rubies

Good with the Bad

The Book of Splendor teaches "When you expect the best, you release a magnetic force in your mind which the law of attraction tends to bring to you." I'd like to build upon that thought with "you have to take the good with the bad."

Are you perfect? Is your best perfection? If something is not perfect, it is to say that it has flaws, or a single flaw. Regardless, if something is perfect it is without flaw or blemishes. So if something is the best but is not perfect, then it will still have a flaw or flaws. It may have one single flaw. **To "take the good with the bad" is to accept the best by accepting the single flaw or multiple flaws, understanding that this comes with the best.**

Everyone wants to be Michael Jordan. But does everyone want what comes with being Michael Jordan? I strive to be the master of women so how can I get upset or get mad when I have to battle them or deal with the problems that come with them? It is up to me to govern myself as a gentleman because I understand my situation and the game and goal I play for. **When you expect the best, you bring the things that come with being the best. How you deal with those things determines whether you will stay the best.** It is key to understand that these things could be the flaws and you must accept them with the same open heart so you can defeat them and continue to enjoy the best.

This is another reason why it is important to be mindful of what it is that you seek. You have to recognize that for all the good that something may be, it will have flaws. Don't short yourself by expecting it to be perfect. **Another thing to realize is that sometimes what we assume to be the best is not the best.** This happens because we are not perfect and sometimes we miss the target because of a flaw in our perception or actions.

If you strive to be the Man, you must understand that with that title comes attention, and with attention comes certain interactions, good and bad. You can't get mad at these things because these are things that come with being the Man. You have to learn to take the good with the bad. As soon as you realize these things, you can plan to govern yourself accordingly. Why? You can plan for these things in the future because you understand that they come with success. Now, that which has the potential to be a problem can be accounted for. **You cannot allow these flaws to deter you from enjoying the pleasures of success or the best.**

Stand Strong

Women seek out a strong man, but what is a strong man? How is it that a man shows his strength?

A gentleman of leisure or G.O.L. is a man who defines himself by his character in a way that women choose his company and often pay for it in a manner that the gentleman chooses. Why do women choose him? It is because he stands strong on the belief that he is the best man for the plan. He believes that he has the best plan for the lady and the best way to motivate her to achieve the goal, and he stands strong on this understanding.

Women were created to assist a man in life. "The LORD God said, 'It is not good for the man to be alone. I will make a helper suitable for him...'"(Gen 2:18, the thought the Creator had when he thought of creating Eve). Point blank, period. When a man chooses to court a lady, he should know how this lady will help him achieve some sort of dream. The courting process should consist of selling the woman the dream and the methods on how they as a team would reach the goal together. A gentleman never seeks out a lady just for the benefits of the physical body. The body can only be a means to a bigger goal.

When a woman chooses a man, she chooses what he is doing in life, where he can go, and the greatness he can achieve. It is up to the man to stand strong on these attributes. Stand strong on being whatever it is that you strive to be, and believe in. This is why it is important to understand why the woman wants the man and how she sees him and their future. It is up to the man to make sure these things are aligned with his plan. If they are, and he stands strong on who he is and grows as he is supposed to, then he will have a woman who is loyal. She will be loyal to the strength of his gravitational pull and control. Once she becomes yours, your "strength" will keep her from being taken by another man, or being led astray.

You give the woman what she wants but you give it to her in your own unique way, in a strong manner. That means mentally, physically, and spiritually; you satisfy her by giving her what she seeks in your own way. Once she chooses, it is up to you to stand strong on the dream you sold her. Everything that you do should be done in your certain way in which she can learn to follow and lean upon. That's what women seek when searching for a strong man.

You must have something within yourself that you lean upon so when it is time to stand strong, you have a force within yourself that will sustain you. Examples could be nationalism, religion, philosophies, a career, or a dream. One of the examples or combination of a few would make up the foundation of the strength that you build upon. Through these driving forces, a man would establish the dream and the methodology in which he and the lady would achieve his purpose. Standing strong will force a woman to choose you in a way that causes her to support you in achieving the goal, or she will not have you. Standing strong on who you are will get you the woman you always wanted. Power UP, and "Stand strong on some Pimpin'."

Life Is a Team Game

"Hey, thank you for leaving me off your Mount Rushmore. I'm glad you did. Basketball is a team game, it's not for individual honors. I win back-to-back state championships in high school, back-to-back NCAA championships in college. I won an NBA championship my first year in the league, an NBA championship in my last year, and nine in between. That, Mr. James, is etched in stone."

Bill Russell's comments on Lebron James Top 4 Greatest Basketball Players

I point this out because young people nowadays think they can do everything by themselves. Nothing worth doing is done alone. A person is a student of something, someone, or a combination of both. A person doesn't live and learn by themselves. The people and the method you choose to associate yourself with in life, as you learn and grow, is your team. If you feel you are doing all the right things in life, and you are not winning, maybe you should look at your teammates. WHO YOU GIVE ENERGY TO WILL DIRECTLY DICTATE WHETHER YOU ACHIEVE YOUR GOALS. Yes, I was yelling because you need to hear and understand this point. Bill Russell didn't win those championships by himself; he won them with Red Auerbach. He would not have won without him; they worked as a team. Red, being the coach, had the game plan and Bill Russell had the great ability and the virtue to listen. In return, they won championships.

My last point is this: teamwork takes sacrifice. Everyone on a team sacrifices. They sacrifice for the team goal. The superstar passes the ball to get his teammates involved. He could take the shot, he could try to do it all, but if he gets his teammates involved, he is more likely to win.

Life is a team game. Who you choose to be around will dictate whether or not you win in life. If you choose to be around people who have never tasted the success you seek, how will you get there? If the people you choose to be around have never experienced what you seek, how will they help you get there? If you spend "A" amount of hours working, and "B" amount of hours handling basic day to day chores, then you spend "X" amount of hours with the person or people who can't help you achieve your goal, and you add them up, how much time is that? How much time do you spend with people who can help you get to where you really want to go? Are you winning? Can you count your championship goals that you accomplished and recognize who you achieved them with? Think about who was around you when you achieved your goals in life. Who put you in that position to win? These people are your team. Whether you failed or succeeded, the people around you played a part in the win or loss.

Hear and Don't Hear

How do you deal with a woman's tongue? This is a question that has been asked of me a lot recently. "Governor, how do I deal with the crazy stuff my woman says?" The answer is simple: hear and don't hear. By that, I mean you hear what your woman is saying but it is best not to say anything. My mother raised me with saying "see and don't see, hear and don't hear." It means that you see and hear things, but you don't comment on them or recognize them as your business.

When a woman is using words in a confusing or illogical way, it stands better not to say anything. The best course of action is to nod the head and say okay. Take note of what she is saying and the seriousness in which she is saying it, but do not respond. Do not try to make sense or reason of it because the woman is exhibiting her "crazy" nature. Yes, all woman are crazy and they normally show this by the things they say or how they verbalize their thoughts.

If a man feels the need to exercise his right to say something, he should state his point and be done with it. There is no need to argue with logic or reasoning because it won't work. A woman is in her "crazy" mode, and so reasoning with her will only inflame her.

A man should have a special place that he goes to in his mind when his woman starts talking "crazy," a place in his mind that he can find peace at the same time be able to endure the verbal onslaught that he will be undertaking. A man must resist the temptation to fall into the trap that the woman is setting to get a rise out of him. The suggestion to the man is to let her say her piece and go about your business. Use your energy for action to show and prove truth instead of arguing with words. Power UP.

*By listening, paying attention, and not saying anything too argumentative, a man allows himself to use his actions as a method of punishing a woman for the things she says.

The Game Don't Stop

I recently dealt with a situation where The Player made the decision to take himself out of The Game and go and do his own thing. The lesson I learned from the situation is that The Game doesn't stop for anybody. Just because he left, the goal remained, the urge to win was still present and, ultimately I just had to step up and increase my will to win.

In The Game of Life, players leave, quit, get hurt, and even die. Either way The Player exits The Game, The Game continues. The team cannot afford to languish over a fallen player; it must regroup, refocus and double down on its efforts to ensure victory. Sometimes the fallen player is the adversary that a team can rally around. It also allows for "the next man up" mentality, which means it is time for another player to step and embrace the challenge of being his or her best and play the starting role.

Focusing on the fallen player can be a distraction that is detrimental to the chemistry of the team. The distraction can come in the form of lack of motivation or confidence, questions of loyalty and commitment, possibly even the loss of will. The Player's death or decision to quit are the losses that come with the biggest distractions. The emotional baggage that comes with death can affect team spirit, and quitting hurts the morale and dedication of the team. All have effects on overall gameplay and team chemistry.

Overcoming distractions from the fallen player can easily be done by immersing one's self and the team in The Game. By focusing on The Game and the game plan, the team can unite around a common cause and focus on the objective. By recognizing the importance of The Game and their roles in the game plan, the team can use a "loss" for motivation and fuel to get a win. All the raw emotion and energy that is built up within The Player from the loss of their teammate should be released within The Game and exhibited in efforts to succeed, not for selfish play or distraction.

Even if your sidekick is no longer available, The Game is still on. The Game doesn't stop for anyone. There may be a timeout or a break, but The Game will quickly resume. The Player must recognize The Game goes on so they do not get caught up in the distraction of the lost player and get left behind. They must see that the loss of another is an opportunity for them to reach the next level by reaching down and giving 110%. The Game does not stop, and the loss of a teammate is an opportunity for the team to better themselves. Power UP.

Appendix A – The Willy Lynch Letter

This letter is not meant to be taken literally, necessarily. But if one should recognize that the behaviors looked upon were found to be true and the methods are not out of the realm of possibility, the reader could view the letter as having significant historical meaning, in thought and in action.

Willie Lynch letter: The Making of a Slave

http://www.finalcall.com/artman/publish/Perspectives_1/Willie_Lynch_letter_The_Making_of_a_Slave.shtml

This speech was said to have been delivered by Willie Lynch on the bank of the James River in the colony of Virginia in 1712. Lynch was a British slave owner in the West Indies. He was invited to the colony of Virginia in 1712 to teach his methods to slave owners there.

[beginning of the Willie Lynch Letter]

Greetings,

Gentlemen. I greet you here on the bank of the James River in the year of our Lord one thousand seven hundred and twelve. First, I shall thank you, the gentlemen of the Colony of Virginia, for bringing me here. I am here to help you solve some of your problems with slaves. Your invitation reached me on my modest plantation in the West Indies, where I have experimented with some of the newest, and still the oldest, methods for control of slaves. Ancient Rome would envy us if my program is implemented. As our boat sailed south on the James River, named for our illustrious King, whose version of the Bible we cherish, I saw enough to know that your problem is not unique. While Rome used cords of wood as crosses for standing human bodies along its highways in great numbers, you are here using the tree and the rope on occasions. I caught the whiff of a dead slave hanging from a tree, a couple miles back. You are not only losing valuable stock by hangings, you are having uprisings, slaves are running away, your crops are sometimes left in the fields too long for maximum profit, you suffer occasional fires, your animals are killed. Gentlemen, you know what your problems are; I do not need to elaborate. I am not here to enumerate your problems; I am here to introduce you to a method of solving them. In my bag here, I HAVE A FULL PROOF METHOD FOR CONTROLLING YOUR BLACK SLAVES. I guarantee every one of you that, if installed correctly, IT WILL CONTROL THE SLAVES FOR AT LEAST 300 HUNDRED YEARS. My method is simple. Any member of your family or your overseer can use it. I HAVE OUTLINED A NUMBER OF DIFFERENCES AMONG THE SLAVES; AND I TAKE THESE DIFFERENCES AND MAKE THEM BIGGER. I USE FEAR, DISTRUST AND ENVY FOR CONTROL PURPOSES. These methods have worked on my modest plantation in the West Indies and it will work throughout the South. Take this simple little list of differences and think about them. On top of my list is "AGE," but it's there only because it starts with an "a." The second is "COLOR" or shade. There is INTELLIGENCE, SIZE, SEX, SIZES OF PLANTATIONS, STATUS on plantations, ATTITUDE of owners, whether the slaves live in the valley, on a hill,

East, West, North, South, have fine hair, course hair, or is tall or short. Now that you have a list of differences, I shall give you an outline of action, but before that, I shall assure you that DISTRUST IS STRONGER THAN TRUST AND ENVY STRONGER THAN ADULATION, RESPECT OR ADMIRATION. The Black slaves after receiving this indoctrination shall carry on and will become self-refueling and self-generating for HUNDREDS of years, maybe THOUSANDS. Don't forget, you must pitch the OLD black male vs. the YOUNG black male, and the YOUNG black male against the OLD black male. You must use the DARK skin slaves vs. the LIGHT skin slaves, and the LIGHT skin slaves vs. the DARK skin slaves. You must use the FEMALE vs. the MALE, and the MALE vs. the FEMALE. You must also have white servants and overseers [who] distrust all Blacks. But it is NECESSARY THAT YOUR SLAVES TRUST AND DEPEND ON US. THEY MUST LOVE, RESPECT AND TRUST ONLY US. Gentlemen, these kits are your keys to control. Use them. Have your wives and children use them, never miss an opportunity. IF USED INTENSELY FOR ONE YEAR, THE SLAVES THEMSELVES WILL REMAIN PERPETUALLY DISTRUSTFUL. Thank you gentlemen."

LET'S MAKE A SLAVE

It was the interest and business of slave holders to study human nature, and the slave nature in particular, with a view to practical results. I and many of them attained astonishing proficiency in this direction. They had to deal not with earth, wood and stone, but with men and, by every regard, they had for their own safety and prosperity they needed to know the material on which they were to work, conscious of the injustice and wrong they were every hour perpetuating and knowing what they themselves would do. Were they the victims of such wrongs? They were constantly looking for the first signs of the dreaded retribution. They watched therefore with skilled and practiced eyes, and learned to read with great accuracy, the state of mind and heart of the slave, through his sable face. Unusual sobriety, apparent abstractions, sullenness and indifference indeed, any mood out of the common was afforded ground for suspicion and inquiry. Frederick Douglas LET'S MAKE A SLAVE is a study of the scientific process of man-breaking and slave-making. It describes the rationale and results of the Anglo Saxons' ideas and methods of insuring the master/slave relationship. LET'S MAKE A SLAVE "The Original and Development of a Social Being Called 'The Negro.'" Let us make a slave. What do we need? First of all, we need a black nigger man, a pregnant nigger woman and her baby nigger boy. Second, we will use the same basic principle that we use in breaking a horse, combined with some more sustaining factors. What we do with horses is that we break them from one form of life to another; that is, we reduce them from their natural state in nature. Whereas nature provides them with the natural capacity to take care of their offspring, we break that natural string of independence from them and thereby create a dependency status, so that we may be able to get from them useful production for our business and pleasure.

CARDINAL PRINCIPLES FOR MAKING A NEGRO

For fear that our future generations may not understand the principles of breaking both of the beast together, the nigger and the horse. We understand that short range planning economics results in periodic economic chaos; so that to avoid turmoil in the economy, it requires us to have breadth and depth in long range comprehensive planning, articulating both skill sharp perceptions. We lay down the following principles for long range comprehensive economic planning. Both horse and niggers [are] no good to the economy in the wild or natural state. Both must be BROKEN and TIED together for orderly production. For orderly future, special and particular attention must be paid to the FEMALE and the YOUNGEST offspring. Both must be CROSSBRED to produce a variety and division of labor. Both must be taught to respond to a peculiar new LANGUAGE. Psychological and physical instruction of CONTAINMENT must be created for both. We hold the six cardinal principles as truth to be self-evident, based upon following the discourse concerning the economics of breaking and tying the horse and the nigger together, all inclusive of the six principles laid down above. NOTE: Neither principle alone will suffice for good economics. All principles must be employed for orderly good of the nation. Accordingly, both a wild horse and a wild or natur[al] nigger is dangerous even if captured, for they will have the tendency to seek their customary freedom and, in doing so, might kill you in your sleep. You cannot rest. They sleep while you are awake, and are awake while you are asleep. They are DANGEROUS near the family house and it requires too much labor to watch them away from the house. Above all, you cannot get them to work in this natural state. Hence, both the horse and the nigger must be broken; that is breaking them from one form of mental life to another. KEEP THE BODY, TAKE THE MIND! In other words, break the will to resist. Now the breaking process is the same for both the horse and the nigger, only slightly varying in degrees. But, as we said before, there is an art in long range economic planning. YOU MUST KEEP

YOUR EYE AND THOUGHTS ON THE FEMALE and the OFFSPRING of the horse and the nigger. A brief discourse in offspring development will shed light on the key to sound economic principles. Pay little attention to the generation of original breaking, but CONCENTRATE ON FUTURE GENERATION. Therefore, if you break the FEMALE mother, she will BREAK the offspring in its early years of development; and when the offspring is old enough to work, she will deliver it up to you, for her normal female protective tendencies will have been lost in the original breaking process. For example, take the case of the wild stud horse, a female horse and an already infant horse and compare the breaking process with two captured nigger males in their natural state, a pregnant nigger woman with her infant offspring. Take the stud horse, break him for limited containment. Completely break the female horse until she becomes very gentle, whereas you or anybody can ride her in her comfort. Breed the mare and the stud until you have the desired offspring. Then, you can turn the stud to freedom until you need him again. Train the female horse whereby she will eat out of your hand, and she will in turn train the infant horse to eat out of your hand, also. When it comes to breaking the uncivilized nigger, use the same process, but vary the degree and step up the pressure, so as to do a complete reversal of the mind. Take the meanest and most restless nigger, strip him of his clothes in front of the remaining male niggers, the female, and the nigger infant, tar and feather him, tie each leg to a different horse faced in opposite directions, set him afire and beat both horses to pull him apart in front of the remaining niggers. The next step is to take a bullwhip and beat the remaining nigger males to the point of death, in front of the female and the infant. Don't kill him, but PUT THE FEAR OF GOD IN HIM, for he can be useful for future breeding.

An FCN Historical Analysis

THE BREAKING PROCESS OF THE AFRICAN WOMAN

Take the female and run a series of tests on her to see if she will submit to your desires willingly. Test her in every way, because she is the most important factor for good economics. If she shows any sign of resistance in submitting completely to your will, do not hesitate to use the bullwhip on her to extract that last bit of [b----] out of her. Take care not to kill her, for in doing so, you spoil good economics. When in complete submission, she will train her offsprings in the early years to submit to labor when they become of age. Understanding is the best thing. Therefore, we shall go deeper into this area of the subject matter concerning what we have produced here in this breaking process of the female nigger. We have reversed the relationship; in her natural uncivilized state, she would have a strong dependency on the uncivilized nigger male, and she would have a limited protective tendency toward her independent male offspring and would raise male offsprings to be dependent like her. Nature had provided for this type of balance. We reversed nature by burning and pulling a civilized nigger apart and bullwhipping the other to the point of death, all in her presence.

By her being left alone, unprotected, with the MALE IMAGE DESTROYED, the ordeal caused her to move from her psychologically dependent state to a frozen, independent state. In this frozen, psychological state of independence, she will raise her MALE and female offspring in reversed roles. For FEAR of the young male's life, she will psychologically train him to be MENTALLY WEAK and DEPENDENT, but PHYSICALLY STRONG. Because she has become psychologically independent, she will train her FEMALE offsprings to be psychologically independent. What have you got? You've got the nigger WOMAN OUT FRONT AND THE nigger MAN BEHIND AND SCARED. This is a perfect situation of sound sleep and economics. Before the breaking process, we had to be alertly on guard at all times. Now, we can sleep soundly, for out of frozen fear his woman stands guard for us. He cannot get past her early slave-molding process. He is a good tool, now ready to be tied to the horse at a tender age. By the time a nigger boy reaches the age of sixteen, he is soundly broken in and ready for a long life of sound and efficient work and the reproduction of a unit of good labor force. Continually through the breaking of uncivilized savage niggers, by throwing the nigger female savage into a frozen psychological state of independence, by killing the protective male image, and by creating a submissive dependent mind of the nigger male slave, we have created an orbiting cycle that turns on its own axis forever, unless a phenomenon occurs and re-shifts the position of the male and female slaves. We show what we mean by example. Take the case of the two economic slave units and examine them close.

THE NEGRO MARRIAGE

We breed two nigger males with two nigger females. Then, we take the nigger male away from them and keep them moving and working. Say one nigger female bears a nigger female and the other bears a nigger male; both nigger females—being without influence of the nigger male image, frozen with a independent psychology—will raise their offspring into reverse positions. The one with the female offspring will teach her to be like herself, independent and negotiable (we negotiate with her, through her, by her, negotiates her at will). The one with the nigger male offspring, she being frozen subconscious fear for his life, will raise him to be mentally dependent and weak, but physically strong; in other words, body over mind. Now, in a few years when these two offsprings become fertile for early reproduction, we will mate and breed them and continue the cycle. That is good, sound and long range comprehensive planning.

WARNING: POSSIBLE INTERLOPING NEGATIVES

Earlier, we talked about the non-economic good of the horse and the nigger in their wild or natural state; we talked out the principle of breaking and tying them together for orderly production. Furthermore, we talked about paying particular attention to the female savage and her offspring for orderly future planning, then more recently we stated that, by reversing the positions of the male and female savages, we created an orbiting cycle that turns on its own axis forever unless a phenomenon occurred and re-shifts positions of the male and female savages. Our experts warned us about the possibility of this phenomenon occurring, for they say that the mind has a strong drive to correct and re-correct itself over a period of time if it can touch some substantial original historical base; and they advised us that the best way to deal with the phenomenon is to shave off the brute's mental history and create a multiplicity of phenomena of illusions, so that each illusion will twirl in its own orbit, something similar to floating balls in a vacuum. This creation of multiplicity of phenomena of illusions entails the principle of crossbreeding the nigger and the horse as we stated above, the purpose of which is to create a diversified division of labor; thereby creating different levels of labor and different values of illusion at each connecting level of labor. The results of which is the severance of the points of original beginnings for each sphere illusion. Since we feel that the subject matter may get more complicated as we proceed in laying down our economic plan concerning the purpose, reason and effect of crossbreeding horses and niggers, we shall lay down the following definition terms for future generations. Orbiting cycle means a thing turning in a given path. Axis means upon which or around which a body turns. Phenomenon means something beyond ordinary conception and inspires awe and wonder. Multiplicity means a great number. Means a globe. Crossbreeding a horse means taking a horse and breeding it with an ass and you get a dumb, backward, ass long-headed mule that is not reproductive nor productive by itself. Crossbreeding niggers mean taking so many drops of good white blood and putting them into as many nigger women as possible, varying the drops by the various tone that you want, and then letting them breed with each other until another circle of color appears as you desire. What this means is this: Put the niggers and the horse in a breeding pot, mix some asses and some good white blood and what do you get? You got a multiplicity of colors of ass backward, unusual niggers, running, tied to backward ass long-headed mules, the one productive of itself, the other sterile. (The one constant, the other dying, we keep the nigger constant for we may replace the mules for another tool) both mule and nigger tied to each other, neither knowing where the other came from and neither productive for itself, nor without each other.

CONTROLLED LANGUAGE

Crossbreeding completed, for further severance from their original beginning, WE MUST COMPLETELY ANNIHILATE THE MOTHER TONGUE of both the new nigger and the new mule, and institute a new language that involves the new life's work of both. You know language is a peculiar institution. It leads to the heart of a people. The more a foreigner knows about the language of another country the more he is able to move through all levels of that society. Therefore, if the foreigner is an enemy of the country, to the extent that he knows the body of the language, to that extent is the country vulnerable to attack or invasion of a foreign culture. For example, if you take a slave, if you teach him all about your language, he will know all your secrets, and he is then no more a slave, for you can't fool him any longer, and BEING A FOOL IS ONE OF THE BASIC INGREDIENTS OF ANY INCIDENTS TO THE MAINTENANCE OF THE SLAVERY SYSTEM. For example, if you told a slave that he must perform in getting out "our crops" and he knows the language well, he would know that "our crops" didn't mean "our crops" and the slavery system would break down, for he would relate on the basis of what "our crops" really meant. So you have to be careful in setting up the new language; for the slaves would soon be in your house, talking to you as "man to man" and that is death to our economic system. In addition, the definitions of words or terms are only a minute part of the process. Values are created and transported by communication through the body of the language. A total society has many interconnected value systems. All the values in the society have bridges of language to connect them for orderly working in the society. But for these language bridges, these many value systems would sharply clash and cause internal strife or civil war, the degree of the conflict being determined by the magnitude of the issues or relative opposing strength in whatever form. For example, if you put a slave in a hog pen and train him to live there and incorporate in him to value it as a way of life completely, the biggest problem you would have out of him is that he would worry you about provisions to keep the hog pen clean, or the same hog pen and make a slip and incorporate something in his language whereby he comes to value a house more than he does his hog pen, you got a problem. He will soon be in your house.

Additional Note: "Henty Berry, speaking in the Virginia House of Delegates in 1832, described the situation as it existed in many parts of the South at this time: "We have, as far as possible, closed every avenue by which light may enter their (the slaves) minds. If we could extinguish the capacity to see the light, our work would be complete; they would then be on a level with the beasts of the field and we should be safe. I am not certain that we would not do it, if we could find out the process and that on the plea of necessity." From Brown America, The story of a New Race by Edwin R. Embree. 1931 The Viking Press.

Bibliography

Bible Hub: Search, Read, Study the Bible in Many Languages, www.biblehub.com

BrainyQuote. Xplore, March 25, 2015

Burton Stevenson *The Macmillan Book of Proverbs Maxims and Famous Phrases* Macmillan Company, 1968

Greene, Robert,*33 Strategies of War*- Penguin Group for HC and Highbridge Audio for AB. January and April of 2006, New York

... *48 Laws Of Power*,1998 (Viking Press), New York

...*Art of Seduction*-Profile Booksdate 2001, New York

... *Mastery*-Viking Adult November 13,2012, New York

Kabbalah Education Center, Bnei Baruch -edu.kabblah.info

The New Interperters Bible Volume 12- Raymond C. Van Leeuwen Professor of Bible and Theology at Eastern College, St Davids, Pennsylvania, W. Sibley Towner is the Reverand Archbishop McFayden Professor of Biblical Interpretation, Union Theological Seminary in Virgina, Richmond Virgina , Renita Weems is Associate professor of Hebrew Bible, the Divinity School, Vanderbilt University, Nashville Tennessee, Michael Kolarcik , is the Associate Professor, Regis College Toronto, Ontario, Canada, James. Crenshaw is the Robert L. Flowers Professor of Old Testament, Duke University, North Carolina, Richard J. Clifford Professor of Old Testament, Weston School of Theology, Cambridge Mass., Published by Abingdon Press, January 1, 1996

Introducing Communication Theory Analysis and Application-Author(s): Richard West, Lynn H. Turner, published by McGraw-Hill Humanities/Social Sciences/Languages, 2013

Schiffman, Lawerence H.-*The Modern Scholar: The Hebrew Bible* Published by Audiobooks, August 18, 2008, New York

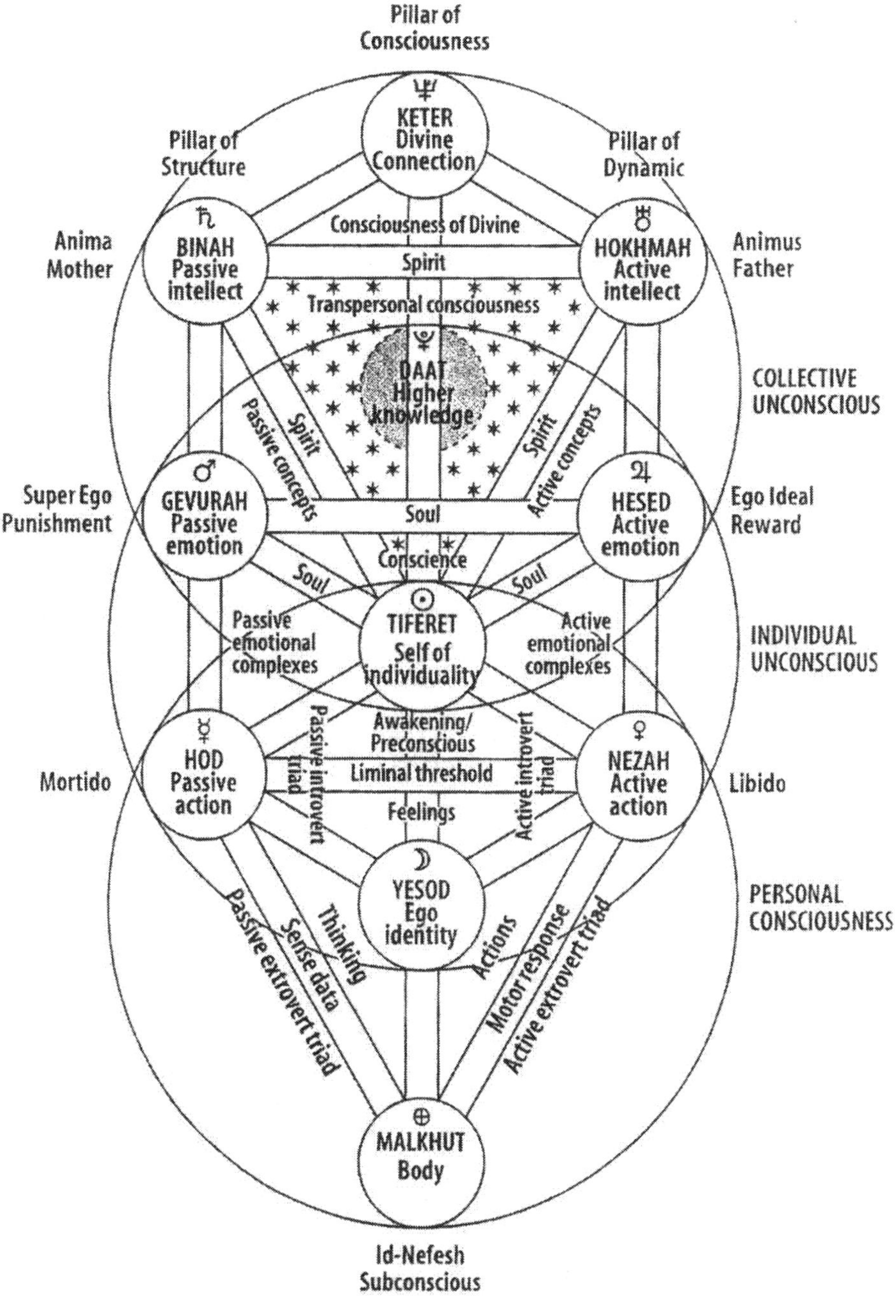
Pillar of Consciousness
KETER
Divine
Connection
Pillar of Structure
Pillar of Dynamic
BINAH
Passive
intellect
HOKHMAH
Active
intellect
Anima
Mother
Animus
Father
Consciousness of Divine
Spirit
Transpersonal consciousness
DAAT
Higher
knowledge
COLLECTIVE
UNCONSCIOUS
Passive concepts
Spirit
Spirit
Active concepts
GEVURAH
Passive
emotion
HESED
Active
emotion
Super Ego
Punishment
Ego Ideal
Reward
Soul
Conscience
Soul
Soul
TIFERET
Self of
individuality
Passive
emotional
complexes
Active
emotional
complexes
INDIVIDUAL
UNCONSCIOUS
HOD
Passive
action
NEZAH
Active
action
Mortido
Libido
Passive introvert triad
Active introvert triad
Awakening/
Preconscious
Liminal threshold
Feelings
YESOD
Ego
identity
PERSONAL
CONSCIOUSNESS
Passive extrovert triad
Sense data
Thinking
Actions
Motor response
Active extrovert triad
MALKHUT
Body
Id-Nefesh
Subconscious

Made in the USA
Lexington, KY
09 December 2019

58327803R00122